ROAD TRIP

A PRACTICAL MANUAL

COVER IMAGE: The Atlantic Road, Norway. *(Shutterstock)*

© Mike Breslin 2020

Map artwork by Barbara Stanley

All rights reserved. No part of this publication may be reproduced or stored in a retrieval system or transmitted, in any form or by any means, electronic, mechanical, photocopying, recording or otherwise, without prior permission in writing from Haynes Publishing.

First published in January 2020

A catalogue record for this book is available from the British Library.

ISBN 978 1 78521 593 3

Library of Congress control no. 2019943428

Published by Haynes Publishing,
Sparkford, Yeovil, Somerset BA22 7JJ, UK.
Tel: 01963 440635
Int. tel: +44 1963 440635
Website: www.haynes.com

Haynes North America Inc.,
859 Lawrence Drive, Newbury Park,
California 91320, USA.

Printed in Malaysia.

ROAD TRIP

A PRACTICAL MANUAL

Inspiration, routes and expert advice for planning and driving road trips around the world

MIKE BRESLIN

CONTENTS

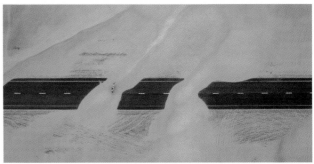

INTRODUCTION

You could argue for hours about what it means exactly to have an adventure. But if you're of the mind that adventure encompasses freedom, new experiences and the unexpected, then road trips fit the bill very well indeed. On top of that, these are the sort of adventures just about anybody can enjoy, without being boiled alive by cannibals, losing a toe through frostbite or drinking your own urine – usually, anyway.

Once you've finished arguing about the meaning of adventure you might start bickering about just what a road trip actually is. It's obviously not a trip to the shops, it has to be more than that. Maybe it needs to be a quest, to research or discover, or perhaps nothing more than a long drive? But for the purpose of this book, and I think in line with the general usage of the term, a road trip is when it's about the journey rather than the destination.

I've refined this a little, so that a road trip here is a journey of at least a few days, in a vehicle or on a motorcycle, in which you stay at a number of different places along the way. Other than that, there are no rules other than those you want to stick to. For, above all else, a road trip is about freedom.

Like many, my first experience of independent travel was backpacking, in Europe and Asia but mostly in North Africa and the Middle East. It was exciting and illuminating, always, and I've covered thousands of miles sharing buses and trains with goats and chickens, but relying on public transport has its limitations. I've always enjoyed driving and so, in retrospect, it's perhaps a little surprising that I didn't combine the two earlier.

We did our first proper road trip (I usually travel with my wife, Jas) well over 20 years ago now, in Germany, and since then we have undertaken road trips on six

continents, which leaves only Antarctica – anyone have a snowmobile we could borrow? In fact, a quick and rough calculation of distance accrued over our road trips came up with a figure of around 36,000 miles (58,000km), which is one and a bit times around the circumference of the earth. Or, to put it another way: right across the USA, Australia and Europe, bits of South America and Asia, and quite a large chunk of Africa.

In these pages I'll recount our own adventures in the hope that some of our experiences – including the mistakes and the few better decisions we've made – will help you to choose and plan a trip of your own. And believe me, if we can do these trips then you certainly can.

Yet so often I hear people say they've always wanted to drive Route 66 or take a campervan across Australia in a 'but it will never happen' sort of way, usually because of lack of time or lack of money. But a proper adventure-filled road trip need not break the bank or use up all your holiday allowance in one go. I hope the trips, and the tips, in these pages will show that.

This book is intended to be about both inspiration and information. The basics are covered first and then I've split the world into six continents, with the slight cheat of merging South America with Central America and a little bit of the Caribbean and calling it Latin America.

Each chapter starts with a feature trip that we've done, then there's a selection of other trips in less detail, though each and every one is backed up with a Planning notes panel and a rough map that should put you on the right road to coming up with your own road trip.

I've driven many of the 50 routes featured in this book, sometimes completely and sometimes in part, but where I haven't I've planned it as if I'm about to – and now I need to! – while also checking the details as thoroughly as is possible. But sometimes things will change over time, so bear that in mind. Many of the trips here we did some years ago now, too – though I've made every effort to make sure the information is up to date – while this book will also date.

But, and this is important, this is not a guidebook. Its purpose is to inspire, I hope, and maybe suggest, but the planning will be down to you – and, like us, you might find that aspect of it one of the most enjoyable parts of the adventure.

One thing I have made an effort to do is to make sure that each and every trip is exactly that; a trip. There are books out there which will itemise some of the world's best drives,

but they never seem to tell you how to get there. It's all very well saying the Sani Pass is one of Africa's great driving challenges, but on a road trip you need to drive to it, before you drive over it. You don't suddenly materialise in Lesotho or the Drakensberg and then disappear once you're the other side. So I've tried to show 'complete' road trips rather than just roads, and when it is the latter I've made an effort to suggest ways to expand it in the Planning notes.

There are as many types of road trips as there are types of roads, and if you enjoy driving – actually, even if you merely tolerate driving or simply don't hate it – then there will be something for you. They range from the easiest fly-drive options that are marketed by travel agents, which include everything from car hire to hotels and can last a week, to full-on independent adventures that might last months.

Categorising trips is tempting. Is it scenic? Is it an adventure? Is it all about history? Or is it about the animals? Problem is, there's always history, often animals, regularly adventure and quite a lot of the time something out of the

window. So I've resisted this, and let the words give you a flavour of what to expect.

One piece of advice here, though: don't forget to stop. Even if it's a trip that's all about the driving, and some are, you really do need to get out of the car and meet people at some point or other; you haven't really seen a place, and you certainly don't know a place, if you've not been in contact with the people. I'd even go as far as to say that it's people that make a road trip, not cars.

You will also often share the road with the past, too, and the best road trips can be journeys through history, and so I have not neglected that where it's pertinent, while there's also just a little bit of philosophy – there's nothing like the wide open road for inspiring reflection, especially in the desert. There are always questions that go beyond 'are we there yet?' on a road trip.

But most importantly, as I said above, a road trip is about freedom. So in the end it's up to you where you go and how you enjoy it. Just drive.

Mike Breslin

Chapter 1

THE BASICS

A road trip is a very simple thing, in essence, but the very best of them will still need a little planning, while if you're taking your car abroad or hiring a vehicle overseas then there are a few things you really should be aware of. So, here are some important points to ponder before you get your motor runnin' and head out on the highway.

There's something intoxicatingly romantic about just getting in your car or on your bike and hitting the road, and then simply going where the highway takes you. But if you're short on time and have a fixed budget then you will want to maximise both of these precious assets, and so planning your route and even your overnight stops will make perfect sense. It might sound a bit boring, but it's the best way to go about getting the most from your road trip, while it can also be an enjoyable process in its own right.

But before you start planning you need to decide exactly where you want to go. This is usually the easy bit – if not then Chapters 2 to 7 will hopefully inspire you. Once you've decided on where you want to do your road trip then these days you will likely do a little research on the internet first, just to get a feel for whether the country or continent you have in mind is really right for you. But to dig a little deeper, the next step should be guidebooks; they cover much more ground than a website or blog, giving you a wider variety of options, and – on the whole – they give solid advice and information.

It makes sense to source guidebooks from a local library to begin with, as they are not cheap and it's not so important that they're fully up to date to start off, while there's always the chance you might change your mind – and there's nothing quite as sad as having a guidebook for a place you've never been to on your bookshelf.

We've found Bradt travel guides are quite well-suited to road trips, but Rough Guides and Lonely Planet also have their plus points. The copiously illustrated DK Eyewitness Travel guides are quite good, too, especially as they tend to have decent maps and good suggested routes. By the way, when it comes to actually purchasing a guidebook when you've fully committed to the trip then it's always worth checking when it was published, and waiting until the new edition is out if its due before you travel, just to make sure all the info you have is as up to date as possible – though there are usually handy updates for guidebooks posted on the internet, too.

Whichever guidebook you use, the highlights section is the first thing to look at, and then the suggested itineraries. As these cover the main points of interest they will help you plan your route in terms of where you want to visit and where you want to spend the most time, which will likely pin down the locations for your overnight stops. But it's also

▼ **How much planning you do is up to you, but if you're short of time or money – or both – then you really should do some.** *(Bresmedia)*

▼ **Guidebooks are a good way to get a taste for the country you want to visit and are great for helping you to devise your route.** *(Bresmedia)*

▲ The reality might not always match the pictures, so check on average temperatures and rainfall at the time of your visit. *(Shutterstock)*

▲ It makes sense to use maps and guidebooks as well as the internet; they all have their own strengths. *(Bresmedia)*

worth reading on in a bit more detail before you commit to the trip, not only to make sure this is definitely the country for you, but also because it's galling to discover there was something you would really have loved to see or do when you've already opted to go to another part of the country, or even when you're at the airport ready to fly home.

Also, make sure you study the sections relating to driving. These can be a bit off-putting sometimes, but double check on the internet too. A couple of the guidebooks said Tanzania is not a self-drive destination, for instance, but we found a company hiring out 4x4s for a fair price and can confirm that it certainly is.

At this early stage another thing you really need to do is check your government's travel advice to make sure the country you're looking at is safe to visit – in the UK this is the FCO, the Foreign and Commonwealth Office (www.gov.uk/foreign-travel-advice).

When to go

Guidebooks will always give you a very good idea of the best time of year to visit a country, and this sort of information is also readily available on the internet. But don't confuse *best* with *only*. There are often some very good reasons to visit a place in the shoulder seasons – which lie between high and low season – and even the low season. The weather might not be at its very best, but on the other hand accommodation can be both cheaper and easier to find, while you won't have to put up with crowds at popular tourist spots either. One thing, though, try out some hotel websites in each place you aim to stay on the dates you're thinking of visiting first, just in case that international shoe painting jamboree is in town at the exact same time as you're planning on going. You'll know if it is, as every hotel will be full, and so you might then want to think of going on your trip at another time if this is a place you really want to see.

It's worth mentioning here that just because the picture on the front of the guidebook shows a slanting palm tree on a sun-kissed beach, that doesn't mean it's hot year round, or at night. Always take a close look at the temperatures and rainfall for the time of your visit before you fully commit to the trip.

With the route slowly crystallising in your head – always exciting – you will now also need to think about time. How much of it will you need to make this a worthwhile road trip and, perhaps more importantly, how much can you spare? This is where compromise might start to rear its ugly head.

Mapping your route

Now you know where you're going, what you want to see and how much time you have, it's time to start planning the route. Not so very long ago this would mean getting hold of some maps or a road atlas, but with websites such as Google Maps and apps that are similar, this is no longer the case.

That said, while the internet is great, you really do know where you are with a map. In fact, we will often do our early planning using one. There's nothing quite like a map spread out on a table to give you an overview – literally – of a country. Things will jump out at you, too: look at that squiggly pass over those mountains; what about this village tucked into that secluded bay; surely by missing out Drabsville we can use this twisting road and go through Puerto Dazzle?

But a map will only go so far, particularly when it comes to estimating driving times, and this is one of the great strengths of mapping sites like Google Maps. In your early planning, the first thing you need to know is how long it's likely to take you to drive between some of the destinations you've picked out, and whether the trip is indeed feasible in the time you have available. One thing, though, if there are big towns or cities in faraway places involved then use the time of departure function, otherwise it will show you how long it will take at the time you've checked, which with the time difference might be the middle of the night in Kyoto or Adelaide, and there's not much traffic around then.

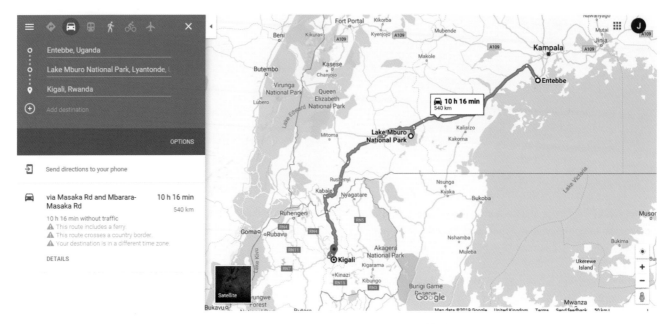

▲ **Google Maps and similar sites have changed the face of road trip planning.** *(Google Maps)*

Also, note that the first location you enter on Google Maps will be treated as a destination rather than a start point, so swap them around before you go to the third destination – using the 'drag to reorder' blobs – to get a neater picture and to make sure the distance total is not confused. It's then easy enough to string together a series of locations and watch the map of your road trip come together before your eyes. Quite exciting, too. As mentioned, there are other sites, such as Bing Maps, MapQuest, maps.me and more.

▼ **You need to remember to factor in time for the many stops to admire the view when planning your days on the road.** *(Greg Snell)*

We've found it's best to plan to arrive somewhere at 3pm at the very latest, which is something we always take into consideration when we're honing our route plan. This gives you a bit of time to see a place if you're just staying a night, while it's also usually quite a few hours before dusk – and in some countries you don't really want to be driving at night-time if you can help it. It's also often around about the earliest check-in time for hotels and motels. We will usually add an hour to the estimated journey time when we're planning, as it will give you both some slack and some time to stop off and see stuff along the way.

All that said, the estimates on Google Maps are not always accurate, though to be fair we've found it usually over-estimates than under-estimates; and sometimes by quite a bit, though this is a country by country thing. Play it safe and add some time for contingencies.

I've seen recommendations in guidebooks that you should try to drive a maximum of 300 to 350 miles (482 to 563km) a day, which is reasonable, and also actually quite far. But it's probably best to think in terms of time. Five to six hours is pretty comfortable, but if you're sharing the driving then all this becomes less of an issue. Taking a break every two or three hours is certainly recommended, though.

Detail planning

Once you have a good idea of the route you want to follow then it's time to pin down your trip. Which, if it's a flyaway, means spending money. This is not the place to go into choosing flights, but it's worth bearing in mind that the times of your flights could easily mean a change to your route; because if it's a long overnight flight to get there are you really comfortable with jumping straight in a hire car and driving in a foreign country? Similarly, if it's an early flight to return, your last stop will have to be near the airport, which could mean losing a day's driving from your initial plan.

With the flight times nailed down, you can now start to work on the detail of the route, and booking the accommodation if that's the way you want to do it, knowing that you can chop and change as much as you like, just so long as you're back at the airport in time to fly home.

We always put together a road book at this stage. It might sound a bit geeky, but it works. It happened by accident at first; too many notes on beermats that then found their way into an exercise book. This soon became a page a day sort of thing, with all the information needed for that day's drive available at the turn of a leaf. Later we started using ring binders so loose documents, like hotel booking confirmations, can be inserted alongside the relevant page. It works very well. We will often have a printout of the directions from Google Maps on the day's spread, too, plus any relevant information we've gleaned from guidebooks or elsewhere while we're planning, such as interesting detours and fuel stop locations.

Bear in mind

On the subject of fuel, petrol stations are important and can be few and far between in some countries, especially if you're travelling in desert or wilderness areas, so you may have to factor this into your planning – charging points for EVs are even fewer and farther between, and if you're thinking of using an electric car this will be the singularly most important aspect of all your planning (we'll go into this in a little more detail later).

Another important detail is the road surface. In some countries there is a mixture of tarmac, gravel and even

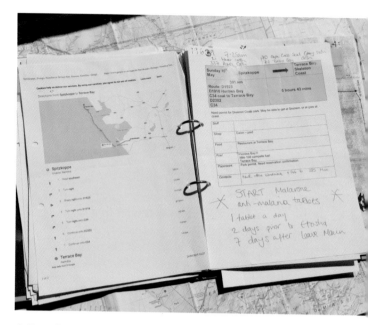

▲ **Page from road book: This contains all the important information for that day.** *(Bresmedia)*

rougher tracks. If you're using a regular vehicle – and especially a sports motorcycle or sports car – then you may be more comfortable taking an alternative, longer but smoother, route rather than risk a puncture or enduring a bone-rattling and possibly car-damaging drive.

The colour of the road on a map should tell you if it's an unpaved track of some sort – usually white is gravel or rough stuff, but check the key. If in doubt, you can always click on the 'Satellite' icon in the lower left corner of the Google Map and then take a look at the photograph of the road from above. This is not always a reliable method as sometimes

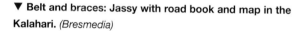

▼ **Belt and braces: Jassy with road book and map in the Kalahari.** *(Bresmedia)*

▼ **This looks great fun but would you really want to do the same in a Ferrari? Try to check the road conditions will be okay for your vehicle as you plan.** *(Tourism and Events Queensland)*

gravel can be the same colour as asphalt, while the image is not always up to date, either. But it's worked for us on many occasions. Streetview is an even better way to get a look at the state of the road surface – just drag the little yellow man from the bottom right corner on to the road – but then this tends not to be available off the beaten track; which is not much good if you need to know just how beaten that track actually is.

Budgeting

Budgets can vary wildly in the same country depending largely on the type of accommodation you opt for, and that, of course, is your choice – the rates are readily available on hotel booking sites and the like. But fuel prices are the same for everybody. Look up the petrol and diesel prices on the internet, and then chuck 10% on top in case of fluctuations or inaccuracies. Europe is the most expensive continent for buying fuel, with Iceland the priciest place to fill up at the time of writing. Not surprisingly, the oil-producing nations tend to be the cheapest – in Venezuela, as I write, petrol was $0.01 a litre (that's less than 1p). But the world's relationship with fossil fuels is changing and more and more governments are now stepping away from the practice of subsiding petrol and diesel and prices are sure to go up in many countries where fuel is currently cheap.

Budgeting for food and drink is simple enough, guidebooks tend to be spot on with this, but if yours is not in date then check on the internet. Searching: 'How much is a meal in …' will usually work well. But bear in mind that because you're on the road you will often find cheaper places for lunch than those that are in the heart of a major city.

The next question is: how do you pay? A little roadside café might not take plastic, for example, and the same goes for petrol stations. This is a country by country thing and very much road trip specific, but as a rule of thumb you can't go too far wrong if you take a mix of cards and sometimes a mix of currencies. But check that you can use your credit or debit card abroad before you leave – one time in Canada mine was declined because I hadn't notified my bank that I was intending on using it overseas, and this is still the case with some cards and banks.

You will obviously need enough local currency and if that can't be exchanged in your home country then make sure you take cash that is easily converted; US dollars are usually the best, but not always, so check. Also, be very careful when arriving in a country that you're aware of just how much a note is worth. It can be confusing for a day or two, especially when it might have a long line of noughts across it. One time, some years ago in Turkey, the inflation was so rampant everything we paid for was in so many million lire. We were given change in the form of ten or 12 coins taped together in stacks to make one, very tall, denomination.

One other thing to do with money; always try to make sure you have some local currency on you, in case of emergencies.

Most of the above is common sense. But that doesn't make it any less relevant. Yet how much you actually plan ahead is very much up to you, and some destinations will require more planning than others, that's for sure. The thing is, planning can be an exciting part of the trip itself, a formalised form of anticipation in some ways. Yet however much you might enjoy preparing for a trip, it's always just the appetiser.

▼ A selection of credit and debit cards is great, and you will also often need some hard cash. *(Shutterstock)*

▼ Small shops like this one in Rwanda will probably not take plastic, so make sure you always have local currency to hand. *(Bresmedia)*

Generally speaking, what you will drive or ride on a road trip will either be your own car or bike, or a rental. To start with the former, you're more likely to find a road trip that suits your car than buy a car that suits a road trip. That's not to say that there's no mileage – pun intended – in the latter option, though. For very big trips which will take months to complete – Highway 1 around Australia, for example – buying a car, truck or camper in the country or continent you're exploring makes perfect sense. It can also make sense if the rental fee, or drop-off charge for a one-way hire, is very high. Hiring a car is particularly expensive if you're young, especially if you are under 25, so, if that's you, a second-hand vehicle can be a much better option. It could also make for more of an adventure.

All that said, if you compare the prices of hiring, including the drop-off fee, with the cost of buying a car, the insurance, and all the taxes and so on, then you will usually find that renting is the better bet if you're only looking at two to three weeks. But if it's anything over a month then it's worth considering buying a used vehicle. One other point – if you've a finite amount of time then bear in mind that buying and selling a vehicle can be a time-consuming process, and do you really want to spend a few days looking for a car, haggling over

▶ Buying a second-hand car for your trip can make sense in the States – but there's lots of paperwork to complete and it will also eat up precious time. *(Shutterstock)*

▲ There's a lot to be said for buying second hand for your road trip if it's to last a month or more – though you might want to thoroughly check the condition of the car before you hand over your money. *(Shutterstock)*

its cost, checking it's okay and then filling in forms when you could be out on the road in a reliable hire car?

The actual process of buying second hand will differ from country to country, but in the United States, to give one example, some of the complications you might face are that you will need an address at which to register the vehicle (and proof of that address), while you will also need insurance (which can be expensive for foreign drivers), and roadside assistance is probably a good idea if you're buying an old car, too. You will also have to register your car with the DMV (Department of Motor Vehicles) and get your own personal licence plates – these are for you and not the car, so they can make great souvenirs at the end of your trip.

Talking of the end of the trip, when this comes you will, of course, want to sell the vehicle on to recoup some of your outlay, which will involve some more paperwork. There are also different rules in each state which you need to be aware of – for instance, there are strict emissions laws in California when it comes to selling vehicles. Most good guidebooks will have a section on buying and selling cars in the country you are visiting, so check this out if this appeals to you.

▲ **We bought this VW Polo for £300 and it took us 6,500 miles (10,500km) around Europe and Turkey with just a couple of minor issues.** *(Bresmedia)*

▼ **It makes sense to get your car serviced before a long road trip, and whatever the distance you should make sure you check the oil and water levels.** *(Shutterstock)*

Another option is to ship your vehicle to the country or continent you want to do your road trip in. This can be a surprisingly inexpensive solution, but on the other hand it can be a surprisingly expensive solution, too. The point is, it is hugely dependent on not just where you want to transport your vehicle to, but also on how flexible you are, and in particular just how long you are willing to be without your car, bike, truck or camper. If you are coming from Europe and you want to use your own vehicle in North or South America or Oceania, this is the only way; but there are also complications around emissions regulations etc. when it comes to shipping a car to another land.

In Africa, south of the Sahara right now, shipping is actually the only way you can do a big trip if you're coming from Europe – though this will, I hope, change – but there are some good shipping deals to be had through the port of Durban, in South Africa.

Vehicle prep

While I wrote above that you're more likely to choose a road trip to suit your vehicle than the other way around, I have actually bought a car just for a specific road trip. Some years ago I acquired an old VW Polo for £300, with the intention of seeing a lot of Europe and much of Turkey on the cheap. It was a Volkswagen because I had a deal to write some features on the trip for a VW magazine, but also because old 'Dubs really are very tough cars indeed. It got us to the heart of Turkey, having driven through France, Switzerland, Italy and Greece and then back through an Eastern Europe that was still in the process of change, with just a couple of small issues – and that was with very little in the way of serious preparation.

We did, however, take some mechanical precautions. A quick service didn't cost much, while it's not too difficult to check the most important things: engine oil; gearbox oil; water; brake fluid; window wash level and wiper blades; tyres; hoses; belts; and lights.

It's also worth planning ahead for emergencies, and while carrying a spare gearbox might be taking it a bit far, headlight bulbs, a can of oil and some gaffer tape will add little weight yet could make a big difference. But try not to overdo it, as you will usually be able to get most of this stuff where you're going, while packing your car and bike well will always be an important consideration.

This is because stuff means weight, and weight stuffs performance. It stresses the vehicle too, while it also means you will have to use more fuel to keep it moving. Whatever sort of road trip it's always advisable to take as little as you can, really, and always weigh up the pros and cons of taking individual items along with you.

A quick word here on extreme weather. We cover desert driving elsewhere in this book, but if you're travelling somewhere where the temperature will dip below 0°C then be prepared for it. Fit winter tyres, and if you have a diesel then make sure you're using winter fuel.

Other vehicle options

Of course, there's no restriction on what vehicle you use on a road trip. But it's when a road trip sometimes becomes an off-road trip that things might need a bit more thought. To get to the really interesting places in Africa, Asia, South America and even Australia, can mean that four-wheel drive or a bike that's good for rough stuff is the way to go. Often, though, what you will really want is the high ground clearance that comes with a 4x4, so a basic SUV will sometimes do the job. All this will need to be decided on when you're planning your route, but if you are making it up as you go along then maybe a 4x4 will cover all the bases.

If freedom really is your thing, then a campervan or motorhome might be for you; or you might even consider towing a caravan. But you need to think long and hard about both of these options. A campervan can be slow, and towing a caravan even slower, and there can be strict restrictions on where you're allowed to take hired campers, in terms of road surfaces. We'll come back to all this in the accommodation section.

▲ **An SUV like this Toyota Rav 4 – about to cross the Tropic of Capricorn in Chile – will give good ground clearance if the going gets rough.** (Bresmedia)

Electric switch

Things are changing in the car world right now, which means soon enough the same will be so for the road trip world as well, so we really do need to consider electric vehicles (EVs). It wasn't so very long ago that you wouldn't even think about doing a road trip in an electric car. These days, however, it's certainly possible – albeit with *very* thorough planning – and it's getting easier all the time. The operating range of electric cars is now being stretched at a remarkable rate. At the time

▼ **Campervans offer freedom and are particularly well-suited to Australian road trips.** (Mitchell Cox/Tourism NT)

▲ **The Tesla Model S has the best range of all electric cars at the time of writing, but even in one of these an EV road trip will take careful planning.** *(Tesla)*

of writing there are eight models of EV available that can go further than 200 miles (320km), while the Tesla Model S is good for 375 miles (600km) and the same company is planning on bringing out a revised version of its Roadster in 2020 that will have a range of 620 miles (1,000km).

But while EVs have come a long way in being able to go a long way, their efficiency is subject to a number of caveats. All the things that will raise fuel consumption on a regular car – driving quickly, carrying loads, hilly terrain and even travelling with the sunroof open – will drain power cells. Also, if the weather's especially hot or cold then this will suck more life out of the battery, both directly or through the use of the energy-draining air conditioning or heating system. All

this comes with the added complication that right now it's unlikely that a charging point will be easy to find, and that's still the real issue here – we will return to this later.

Car hire

If you need to fly to where you're planning on doing your road trip, then a hire car will probably be your preferred option. There are actually some very good reasons to use a hire car anyway, the main one being that you don't have to worry about the wear and tear on your own car, while you will usually get a new or nearly new vehicle – though this is by no means always the case.

Yet while there are obvious advantages to renting a car, the market can be complicated and you will need to research it for the countries you are visiting – most of the main guidebooks are pretty good on this – and also shop around, as prices can vary substantially, even in the same locations.

▼ **It pays to book your hire car beforehand as even busy airports can run out of vehicles; or at least run out of cheap ones.** *(TK Kurikawa/Shutterstock.com)*

▼ **It's essential that you check the terms and conditions carefully – you might be itching to get out on the road but taking time when picking up a hire car can save you grief later.** *(Shutterstock)*

Your first step into the minefield of foreign car hire should be a virtual one. You can of course turn up at an airport and pick up a car on the day of arrival and many do, but I've lost count of the number of times I've seen people having to take huge, expensive cars or being turned away even at major hubs because there are no vehicles left. It's best to sort it on the internet first.

There are numerous broker websites now, so it's a lot easier to get a competitive deal than it once was. That said, it's always worth taking a deal that offers late cancellation, typically within 24 or 48 hours before collecting your car; that way you can shop around nearer your date of travel and maybe find a late deal that's even better than your original one.

One thing you do need to be careful of is add-on extras such as a service charge; check the small print thoroughly before you arrive and once again when you're picking up the vehicle. And make sure you've made it clear on the form that you're not interested in any optional extras; if you're not. You will often need to have a credit card, too, so as you can leave a security deposit – in the form of a hold on the card – which will cover the excess you might need to pay in the event of an accident.

If you can, and assuming you're flying in, get an in-terminal deal. Those outside the main terminals can be on a hard to find industrial site or a long taxi ride away. Actually, picking up the car at the airport, even if you're staying a day or two in the city before you start your road trip, makes sense if you're not comfortable driving in what can be hectic streets, or if it's difficult to park in the city, as the airport is usually well out of town. So why not have your day or two in the city, and then travel back to the airport to pick up the car and then start your road trip properly from there?

Another thing you will need to check is the fuel policy. The best is full when you pick it up, and full when you drop it off. Then, all you need to remember is to fill it up at the end of your trip. A full to empty policy, on the other hand, works out expensive, as you pay for the full tank and you're unlikely to actually bring it back empty, while what fuel the company will charge you for will be quite expensive, especially once the inevitable service charge is added.

If you're looking at a basic economy car just to bring the price down, then one tip is to book a four-door. These always go first, so if you insist on the four-door you booked, when you're told they are out of them the company will probably upgrade you – but only accept an upgrade if it's free, and in these circumstances it should be, and get something on paper to confirm this, too. Actually, one-way drop-off hires can also often result in an upgrade to a bigger car, but it's a risk – unless you're happy to drive 3,000 miles (5,000km) in a city car.

▲ **One-way drop-offs are a necessary evil if you're hiring for linear trips like Route 66 – yes, Harleys can be hired too.** *(Shutterstock)*

One-way drop-offs are necessary for some of the very best road trips, including Route 66. These can be expensive, but it differs from country to country, yet often you will simply just have to take the hit if you want to do a linear trip. On this subject, it's actually possible to get relocation deals in some countries, where you can drive a hire car that's been dropped off by some other punter back to its home. These one-way relocation services (such as Transfercar in Australia) can be very cost effective, as little as a dollar a day in fact, but they tie you down to where the car needs to be and when it needs to be there. But if you're not set on any one route and you're flexible on dates, then this might be a simple solution when it comes to car hire, and it's almost certainly the cheapest option.

Insurance extras

Where car hire can get really complicated is with the extra insurance cover that can be on offer. This tends to be mentioned just as you're picking up the car, where you will be informed that while the collision damage waiver (CDW) that's part of the hire price will cover you for major damage, you will still be liable for, for example, the first £2,000 in repair costs. Many will panic and fork out for the extra insurance, which can easily double the cost of the car.

The way around this is to get hold of an excess insurance policy before you even fly away. These are relatively cheap and tend to last a year so can cover a number of trips (though they could be limited to a trip that lasts a month at most, so check). There are plenty of companies now offering these policies, which can be found easily with a quick internet search.

Of course, being insurance it's not quite that simple, and another complication is that because you're refusing their extra insurance the hire car provider will then put a block on your credit card to make sure you fork out for the excess should the worst happen. It then becomes a case of getting the excess insurer to sort this out with the rental company later on; if the car is damaged.

With all the above in mind, it's worth taking a few pictures of the car when you return it, just in case of false claims by the hire firm. That said, I've hired cars all over the world and have had very few problems; most firms – like most people – are fair and honest.

There are certain things you should do just in case you are dealing with a dishonest one, though, and much of this is common sense. When collecting the car you need to stick to your guns if you're aggressively being sold the extra insurance (assuming you're fully covered anyway); make sure you study the contract carefully; don't pay for extra breakdown cover if this is already part of the deal; and take pictures of any scratches and dents you've noticed and marked up on the form. Also, make sure you know how the tolls are paid; are you responsible or is it an automatic electronic system – increasingly the case these days – and if it is the latter, do you then need to settle up with the hire car provider when you return the vehicle?

Pick up and drop off

It goes without saying that when you pick the car up you really should give it a thorough inspection. In the past I've been a bit rubbish at this, I always want to get on the move, and one time in Ireland this almost backfired spectacularly. It was raining heavily, and the car simply went straight on at a roundabout. We missed the high kerb by inches, and when I parked up later I realised the front left tyre was completely bald. Talking of tyres, you need to check you have a spare, too, and that it's in good condition, and that there's a jack.

Another important thing, always make sure you know where the petrol cap is and how to open it, and double check whether it's petrol or diesel (it will usually say on the cap anyway, but it might be in another language or even in Japanese or Arabic script). Oh, and if it's a part-time 4wd car, make sure you know how to select it and deselect it, too – this can be complicated on the older trucks that are part of some fleets.

On returning the vehicle give yourself plenty of time, don't leave it to the last minute because any delays could mean you end up paying for an extra day – in extreme cases – while you will also need time to make sure all's in order with the paperwork etc. If there's no one there and you're just dropping off the car and posting the keys – which does happen – then again you might want to make sure you take photos of the car, just to prove all was fine and dandy when you finished with it.

Even if there is 'damage' don't pay up straight away. Check first. One time we dropped off a car at Lyon airport and we were told we had to fork out for a black mark on the white bumper. But then I just rubbed it off with my handkerchief…

One thing to look out for if you're hiring in Africa is that quite often there will be a clause in the contract that says you have to pay for *all* the damage should you overturn the car or truck and there is no other vehicle involved. This is because it's such a common occurrence, especially on the fast gravel roads of Namibia, but in other countries, too.

▼ **Check the condition of the tyres on your hire car, including the spare, and check there's a jack, too.** *(Bresmedia)*

▼ **Make sure you give yourself plenty of time when returning your hire car.** *(Shutterstock)*

Accommodation

With the wheels sorted, the next thing to look at is somewhere to sleep. But whatever your choice of accommodation the first question you will need to address is whether you should book ahead or not. You might not really want to, and that's understandable. There's something exciting about not knowing where you will spend the next night and also knowing that you can just keep driving, or stop where you like, as the mood takes you – this is particularly so in the US, I find, which with its motels is well-suited to this approach.

On the other hand, booking ahead means you have more time for driving and seeing, exactly what you've come for – after spending four hours trying to find a bed in Bratislava some years ago I will now often try to book before I arrive, especially given how easy it is to do so on the internet these days. Of course, the other option is a combination of the two; booking ahead *as* you travel, maybe selecting your accommodation a day or two before you arrive.

In our experience, the internet booking sites are pretty reliable, though sometimes you need to treat the reviews with a pinch of salt – the web has sparked an evolutionary mutation, a subspecies of homo sapiens that thrives on whingeing, so bear that in mind. I can only actually remember one time when a room we'd booked on one of the main sites was not there for us when we turned up. This was a while back in Croatia, but it was a mistake the hotel had made and we ended up with an upgrade.

Of course, one thing you will need if you're on a road trip is somewhere to park the car or the bike, so make sure you put that into the search terms, especially if it's in a city

▲ Staying in an old motel is an essential part of the US road trip experience. This is the Palomino Motel in Tucumcari, New Mexico, on Route 66. It opened in 1939.
(StockPhotoAstur / Shutterstock)

centre. But if you want to check out the parking situation before you arrive at a hotel (motels, of course, are all about parking) then find it on Google Maps, switch to the satellite view and zoom in. It's like having your very own spy satellite. Parking space can be very precious in some cities, so make sure you address this in the planning, or you might end up paying a hefty bill.

It's always much easier to find accommodation – whether booking ahead or turning up on the day – if you're travelling in the off-season or the shoulder season. That said, sometimes campsites in particular might be shut in the winter, so bear this in mind.

▼ If you're staying in a city then you will need to think about parking. This can be an issue in Japan, where this is a common paid-parking method. *(Bresmedia)*

▼ Another solution to parking in Japan is 'car vending machines' like this one at a Nara hotel. *(Bresmedia)*

▲ Camping makes perfect sense on a road trip and it can save you a heap of money. *(Bresmedia)*

▲ It might not be quite as cosy as a campervan but staying in a roof tent is great fun. *(Bresmedia)*

▼ Putting up a roof tent is very easy indeed. It must be, I can do it! *(Bresmedia)*

Camping

If it's true freedom you're after then camping has to be the ideal, though you need to be aware that simply stopping and setting up a tent might not be allowed in some countries and, unless you're obviously in the wildest of wildernesses, you should really ask for permission before bivouacking on someone's land.

In the majority of countries you are most likely to set up your tent in a campsite anyway. These vary, of course, but the best will offer clean ablutions blocks, maybe a laundry and sometimes an on-site bar or restaurant. The worst will offer a patch of dirt, and not much else, but then that's all you really need and it's amazing how often the 'worst' site can offer the best experience.

While you can't check out a campsite before you leave home – beyond reviews on the internet – you can, and most certainly should, check out your equipment. If you're bringing your own tent then make sure you know how to set it up and also spend a night or two in it before the trip. And think about the weather. A tent I once owned had done one trip to Le Mans, where it had been great … but it hadn't rained that year. When we set it up in Italy there was a thunderstorm, and it wasn't quite as waterproof as the label made out. It's nice to have running water at a campsite, but it's not so nice to have it running onto your head. All night.

The same advice goes for camping equipment, such as stoves; practise on a tin of beans before you leave home. Incidentally, I always take little pillboxes of chilli powder, ground black pepper and salt for cooking. It saves having to buy heavy bags of stuff you will not use.

If you're hiring an equipped truck or a campervan there will be a briefing before you set off. The company from which we hired a VW Crafter for an Australian trip even had a video on its website which we could watch a few times before we left for Australia, which showed you how to empty the toilet cartridge, use the fold-out barbeque, set up the beds and so on.

If you're picking up a prepared truck in Africa, it can take a good two hours to go through all the equipment and

how to use it: the Engel fridge; compressor for tyres (you let them down for sand driving); high lift jack; gas cylinder and hob; roof tent and so on – a roof tent is actually very easy to set up, by the way, once you get used to it.

It is important you pay attention, though. When we picked up a Nissan 4x4 in Johannesburg for one trip I didn't fully concentrate on how the single hob gas cooker worked as I'd used something similar in Australia the year before. I must have looked a real idiot at our first campsite when flames were shooting out from under the hob, almost searing my hands, after I'd tightened it in place, then loosened it a little, just as I had with the cooker in Oz. I still don't know why I kept on doing it…

If you are doing an African road trip then camping in a game park will be a highlight. In South Africa and Namibia these tend to be fenced off – though not all of them – but in other countries the animals are allowed to come and go as they please. Apparently, wild animals won't rip through a tent – I'm sure they could if they wanted to, maybe they just don't like their supper wrapped? But make sure you zip up the opening and try not to drink too much before you go to bed; you don't really want to be making a midnight trip to the toilet if there's a leopard lurking round the latrines.

To be honest, though, it's actually quite a thrill to come across a wild animal in your campsite; I came face to face with a huge hyena one night in Tanzania when going to clean my teeth, and on another occasion a lone buffalo – the most unpredictable and hence dangerous of African beasts.

On the subject of hyenas and other wild animals – and not just in Africa – don't leave food around outside when you turn in. Lock it up somewhere safe in the car or truck. Not just food, either; I've heard that hyenas have been known to crunch their way through camera lenses that have been left unattended. They will, literally, eat anything.

I'm not sure campfires actually keep animals away, but they warm the soul and it's great to cook on them. You need to be careful about the wood you use, this is both for ecological reasons and for safety – some woods can produce harmful fumes and lots of smoke when burned. Very often you can buy bundles of firewood for a small fee at the park or campsite gate and this is definitely the way to go.

Campervans

The most comfortable way to camp is to take your home with you. A campervan, motorhome or recreational vehicle (RV) also means great flexibility; if you're stuck for a place to stay you can always stop just about anywhere (within reason), cook your own food and then get some sleep.

Many campervans will be bigger than a car, so if you've not at least hired a van before you will need to take some time to get used to your vehicle; especially if it's a huge

▲ Cooking in the bush – always remember to pack small packs of spices etc. *(Bresmedia)*

▲ Make sure you always lock food away when camping, otherwise wild animals might come visiting. This baboon found something tasty in the bin in Tanzania. *(Bresmedia)*

▼ For many, campervans offer the very best in road trip freedom. We hired this very comfortable VW Crafter in Australia a few years ago. *(Bresmedia)*

▲ Care should be taken when loading a camper and beware of crosswinds in the desert and when crossing bridges.
(Graeme Murray / Tourism New Zealand)

American RV. They're not hard to drive, though, and you shouldn't worry too much, but you do need to take the size of the vehicle into consideration, not only on the road itself but when planning your trip. Some of those enticing winding roads may look like great fun, but are they really suitable for an RV or even a camper? Also, think about your satnav. Remember that these are mainly designed with cars in mind and while this is less of an issue in the States, in Europe they could take you down narrow country lanes – with this in mind check out *Big Road Atlas for Europe*, which shows the wider roads while also warning of low bridges and similar hazards.

While planning will take a little care then, so will loading the van. If you're hiring then try to take luggage that collapses down and can be easily stowed away, and if you have any heavy items of equipment then place them over the axles of the vehicle, while also avoiding too much weight over the front or the rear. You really want it as well balanced as possible.

On the subject of packing, when you set out in the morning make sure everything's stowed away nice and snug and all the doors are shut tight; a banging cupboard door can drive you crazy over a 300 mile (480km) drive, while things might also fall out and break if you're bouncing along a poor road surface.

If you're taking your own camper abroad then make sure you have an adapter so you can hook up to the electricity supply at campsites. Oh, and in any campervan or motorhome you definitely should follow the instructions when it comes to emptying the toilet cassette – you really don't want to be having spillage issues in this department.

Much of the above also applies to caravans – these are beyond the scope of this book but check out *The Caravan Manual*, also by Haynes.

For both caravans and motorhomes there is the extra complication of the wind. These are high sided so this needs to be taken into consideration, especially when negotiating long bridges over open stretches of water or driving across plains or deserts. Also, when overtaking trucks the wind can catch you out. For example, when passing road trains in Australia – and long vehicles don't get much longer than these – the wind off the desert would suddenly hit the camper as we went by, and even though I was expecting it, this was almost always a bit of a shock.

Also, remember you're in a heavier vehicle than a car, it will take more stopping and need more time and distance, so keep even further back from the car in front than you normally would.

Much of what you might take will be covered in the checklist (see Appendix at the end of the book) but one good rule is less is more; more or less. It's easy to take things you will never use, which will just take up more space and add weight. So plan well and pare down. Except when it comes to water. This is especially the case in hotter regions, of course. In fact, if we're crossing a desert we probably take way too much water. But then you will always use it up later in the trip, and it's generally cheap enough. As for food, it's good to have snacks in the car, but also emergency rations – a big bag of nuts and dried fruit is excellent, and cereal bars or energy bars are also good.

Good-quality sunglasses are also important, and for much more than just looking cool, as I found out after sitting on my pair and breaking them on a recent road trip – which is not so cool. With early starts on a long journey you might often find yourself driving into the rising sun and your eyes are important. Go for polarised lenses – which reduce glare – and make sure those lenses actually shield your eyes, while

the frames don't impair your vision. Some brands, Serengeti being a good example, are designed with driving in mind.

In-car entertainment, like music playlists or talking books, is always a personal thing. We used to listen to both, but slowly we found we were only putting on the music in traffic jams, and now rarely at all; mainly because on recent trips there's just been so much to take in. The radio, though, can be fun and informative, especially in the States. But what's not so much fun, but vitally important, is the documentation you will also invariably need to take with you on an international road trip.

Documents

International Driving Permit

Before you get on the road you need a licence, and that's the same pretty much everywhere. Quite often your regular driving licence from home will suffice, but some countries require that you have an International Driving Permit (IDP). The first time I bought one of these was in the late 1980s and I can honestly say that no one has ever asked to see one that I've had since, not when collecting a hire car, at police checkpoints or border crossings. I can also honestly say that having written that, on my very next road trip someone will ask to see it (they did; when I was picking up a hire car!).

But even though they're rarely looked at it would be silly not to get an IDP if a country you're driving in requires that you have one. They are pretty cheap, the price of a pint of beer, and easy to obtain; in the UK they are available from selected post offices (go to www.postoffice.co.uk/international-driving-permit) and the process takes about five minutes over the counter (you need to take your licence and passport and a passport-sized photo that you've signed on the back).

Note here that the IDP is a supplement to your regular licence, and you will still need to take that; in fact, the IDP is

▼ The desert can be a pitiless place so always make sure you have plenty of water. *(Bresmedia)*

▼ Good-quality sunglasses are not just about looking cool. *(Shutterstock)*

▼ Keep important documents somewhere safe, but also make sure they are easy to find if they are needed. *(Shutterstock)*

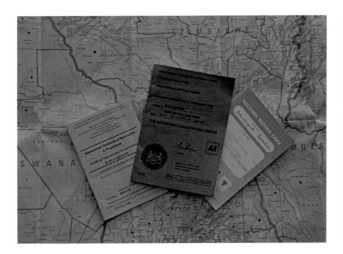

▲ International Driving Permit and vaccination documents. Paperwork is one of the more tiresome aspects of a road trip abroad. *(Bresmedia)*

▲ Classic cars with old-style number plates will need a sticker to show country of origin if they're taken overseas. *(Gary Perkin / Shutterstock)*

only valid if you also have this. If you're in the UK, for a list of countries requiring an IDP go to www.theaa.com, under 'driving advice' and then 'driving abroad'. In other countries your national motoring association should have something similar.

The IDP itself is a little cardboard booklet containing your photo and pages of text in a variety of languages and scripts. You can pre-date these, up to three months, so that they can become valid exactly when you need them and they then last for a year from the validation date.

Proof of ownership

While the licence proves you can drive, you'll also need documents to prove that the vehicle you're at the wheel of really belongs to you. In the UK this is the V5C. You might be asked to show it at a port of entry or if pulled over by the police and if so this must be the original document, not a copy – make sure the address shown on this is up to date too. But where all this gets a little tricky is when you don't actually own the vehicle you're intending to take on a road trip.

If you're taking a vehicle owned by a company, or a borrowed or hired car, abroad, then you will need a letter of authorisation from the registered keeper as well as the original vehicle registration document or a vehicle on hire certificate (in the UK this is a VE103). If it's a leased car, which is becoming all the more common, then you will need permission from the company financing the lease plus a further document from the lease company (in the UK a V103B). You need to sort all this out a few weeks before you go, but your lease provider should be able to tell you exactly what you are required to do. Oh, if it's not already included on your registration plate then a sticker, such as a 'GB' for the UK, will be needed, too.

Other documents you will need will include your motor insurance certificate, and you should check your insurance is

at the same level when you're abroad. At the time of writing, all UK insurance provided a minimum of third party cover throughout the EU. Further afield, a 'green card' is needed to prove the minimum legal cover is in place. With the prospect of political upheaval this might all change, but whatever happens you will still basically need to check with your insurance provider to see what cover you have, and how that might be extended, or if you will need a green card.

Another form of insurance is breakdown recovery. Make sure this is valid for where you're going; you might have to buy an extension to your cover – which is often worth it just for peace of mind. And take the details of your policy with you, as it will be useless if you can't contact anyone if the car breaks down. Sometimes your breakdown cover provider might have a reciprocal agreement with a firm aboard, so it's worth checking this. Hire cars will usually come with their own cover.

Import and export

There is one other piece of paperwork that you might need, especially if you've a very major trip in mind involving your own vehicle, and that's a carnet de passage. This is not the place to go into this in detail, but a carnet is basically a passport for your car, truck or motorbike. It allows you to temporarily import the vehicle into a country without paying customs duty, which can be very expensive. The carnet itself, which is available from national motoring organisations, must be issued in the country in which the vehicle is registered.

If you're looking at an expedition-style road trip in Africa or South America, for instance, using your own vehicle, then this is something you will need to look into, and a good place to start is www.carseurope.net, which is currently registered to issue carnets in the UK after the RAC stopped providing them.

An International Certificate of Motor Vehicles (ICMV) might also be advisable for major trips in your own vehicle. Called the carte grise (grey card, though it's actually white) it's a multilingual booklet that is basically a translation of your vehicle registration documentation into a number of common languages. This is required in many Russian-speaking countries, plus others in Asia and South America, and it's useful enough – and cheap enough – to make it a worthwhile purchase for any big trip. These are valid for 12 months and are usually available through national automobile associations.

Vignettes

Other car documentation you might have to consider include vignettes, in countries such as Switzerland, which you buy at the border. This is a road tax that allows you to use the motorways; and for the price you also get a colourful sticker to put on your windscreen. You can pre-pay for these if you don't fancy buying one at the border and there is plenty of advice online.

One other point on vehicle documentation; some European cities are now restricting access, or levying a charge, for cars that do not meet a certain emissions standard. For instance, if you're planning on driving through Paris, Lille, Grenoble or Lyon in France then you might be hit with a fair-sized fine if you're not displaying a window sticker, also called a vignette, which states your vehicle is clean enough to enter the restricted sector (this is known as the 'Crit'Air' scheme). Note that some vehicles simply won't be able to enter anyway, such as cars registered before 1997 (which might scupper some classic car road trip routes). These stickers can be obtained via the French environment ministry website (www.certificat-air.gouv.fr/en/demande).

This is the sort of thing you really need to look out for at the planning stage of your road trip, as rules and regulations such as these are sure to spread to other cities and towns across the world in the coming years.

▼ If you fancy getting involved in the Paris rush hour then you will need a 'Crit'Air' vignette. (Shutterstock)

▲ A really major road trip/expedition will not only require the proper vehicle, but also the paperwork to allow you to take it to exotic lands. (JuliusKielaitis / Shutterstock)

Personal paperwork

A quick word here on your own documents. In some countries your passport will need to have at least six months' validity left on it, so check this, while you might also require a visa. Often these will be available at the border or the airport but for some nations you will need to obtain them before you leave home, from the embassy of that country. Don't leave this late, as it will mean sending your passport away. Many travel specialists – such as Trailfinders in the UK – will offer a visa service for a cost, which can be helpful. Another piece of paperwork you might need is an inoculations certificate. There are some countries that won't let you enter if you haven't had the jabs for yellow fever, for instance.

Getting the paperwork right before you go will make it much easier to cross borders, turning what can be a hassle into an – almost! – enjoyable adventure …

▼ For some countries you will need to sort a visa before you leave home. (Bresmedia)

Border crossings

You will drive across some borders and you will hardly notice you've done so, but there are other border crossings that will live with you forever. All of the latter type will have their little idiosyncrasies, but one rule will apply everywhere: you need to be patient.

In Europe there are few land borders remaining where you have to stop and show your passport, and when we travelled around the Balkans in 2012 it was actually a bit of a novelty, but elsewhere it can be a bit different, and in Africa taking a car over a border can be an adventure in its own right. Every African border is different, and some are fairly straightforward – South Africa to Namibia and back the other way for instance – but one thing many of the more complex border crossings have in common is fixers.

Fixers, often lads but not always, will walk you through the process for, of course, a fee. It's important to note here that you need to agree on the amount you're willing to pay them before you start, if you choose to use a fixer. From experience I can say that if you don't fix a price, and it's easy to be swept along in the chaos of an African crossing, you'll be storing up trouble for later. These fees don't tend to be high, so try to find out the going rate before you get to the border – sometimes a guidebook will be of help but better still is to talk to someone who's crossed the same border recently.

But do you really need a fixer? It depends on the crossing. For instance, crossing from Zambia into Zimbabwe, although it takes a few hours, is actually quite straightforward

◀ **There's often not much to mark the borders between European countries these days.** *(Shutterstock)*

and logical. But crossing into Zambia from Botswana via the Kazungula ferry is utter madness. It took us two and a half hours with a fixer, and maybe it would have been quite a few more without, as the different offices you need to visit are flung around the compound (this was actually the only time we've felt the need to use a fixer). Also, all the border officials and customs men in Kazungula are dressed like admirals, which made me think someone once, mistakenly, bought a load of uniforms for a Zambian navy and then realised there was no sea. But they take their job seriously, and you would be advised to do the same.

Incidentally, one time, going into Bulgaria, a customs official in an absurd Soviet-style wide-crowned peaked cap spotted the Indian stamps in our passports and decided we'd driven all the way from Delhi. I guess he figured this would have taken us through Afghanistan, as he and his colleague then began to tear the guts out of our car looking, we assumed, for drugs. Mind you, he manged to fix the broken tilting mechanism on the passenger seat as he did so. The reason I tell this tale is that it supports a theory I have; that is that there's a correlation between fancy uniforms and ridiculous hats and problematic border crossings.

But hats and uniforms aside, the really important thing is to make sure you have each and every stamp you need.

▼ **The border crossing between South Africa and Namibia at Mata-Mata is easy to negotiate.**

(Rainer Lesniewski / Shutterstock)

▼ **The Kazungula ferry takes traffic between Botswana and Zambia. There's a bridge being built now which will make it easier; but that's a bit sad too.** *(Bresmedia)*

Here a fixer's help is useful, as they will make sure you've been to every stamp-thumping, form-filling stop. That said, there will usually be a last check before you're through the gate and into the country (make sure you have a 'gate pass'), then often a police checkpoint a little further on, so if you've missed a stop they will simply send you back to finish the process.

Another thing about border crossings; always keep every single piece of paper you're given, and keep it safe. Something that might look like a dry cleaning receipt might make the difference between you being allowed to take your car out of the country or not. We almost had to pay quite a hefty fine once when we couldn't find a tiny slip of paper; but luckily it turned up after we'd emptied the car.

One final word of warning: at a border, people will know for sure you're tourists – sorry, I know, 'adventurers' – and you could be a target for scams. And worse. Once, on a quiet crossing, a heavily armed soldier asked us to pay a 'parking tax'. Luckily, one of the border officials earlier was wise to this and told us we should not pay any further fees, at all, at that post. But don't worry about this too much, the vast majority of people are not out to get you. And that really is the case all over the world.

Checkpoints

Border crossings are not the only barriers you might need to negotiate. Something you might not be used to in your home country is police or military checkpoints, which can be a part of everyday life in some places, particularly in parts of South America and Africa. In Zimbabwe, though this was in Mugabe's time and things might be better now, I think we were stopped 14 times on the road between Victoria Falls and Bulawayo. The advice is the same as it is for borders; stay polite and be patient, and use humour – carefully. When a Zimbabwean policeman told me off for having a mucky truck, I said I'd just come from Botswana, and it's dirty there. That did the trick. I have heard that they 'fine' drivers for having car horns that are too loud in Zim' and other such made-up offences, but we never encountered this.

Complimenting them on their uniform, especially if it's an old colonial style outfit they're a little embarrassed to wear, also helps to make the encounter a whole lot more friendly – just try not to sound sarcastic. Also, if you recognise a rank badge, such as the three sleeve-chevrons of a sergeant, then address them by their rank – that often helps, I find.

In Chile there was another sort of control that we had to stop for, which was a customs post right in the middle of the Atacama Desert and far from any border, which we were certainly not expecting. It was confusing, but the advice is much the same, keep patient and polite, and maybe smile a bit, too.

▲ **Thai police checkpoint close to a border post.** *(Shutterstock)*

BY THE WAY ...

Crossing the line

What is it that makes crossing a line on the map which isn't really even there so exciting? We've crossed the Tropic of Capricorn in a number of countries (Chile, Australia and Namibia) and Cancer in Egypt and Oman. But for the big one, the equator, we had to wait until our most recent trip in Uganda. We took this picture with the truck nice and clean on the way south to Rwanda, and had hoped to have a partner pic when it was dirty on the way back north, but there was no marker of any kind, just road improvement works, which are provided by China. One local told us: 'The Chinese have stolen the equator!'.

Speeding

Of course, the time when you need to be especially friendly towards the authorities is when you've been caught speeding. As I write this, a tourist who hired a Lamborghini Huracan in Dubai has racked up £36,000 in speeding fines – in just four hours. The reason I mention it is because there's a moral to the story; if you don't know the speed limit, then find out – chances are there will be one.

I hesitate to write this, but I have only been caught speeding once in my home country, the UK. But I have been fined in four other separate countries while on road trips; which should tell you something. Rather than go through how fines work country by country, which would need a whole book, I'll run through these, which should provide examples of differing approaches across the globe.

I've been quite lucky and the very first time I was caught speeding was in 2004, more than two decades after I passed my test, and more than 11,000 miles (17,700km) from where I passed it, driving the fantastic road from Queenstown to Milford Sound in New Zealand. The road was empty and reasonably straight and I was in a hire car. I saw another vehicle in the distance coming in the opposite direction and thought little of it, but then when it came a little closer we suddenly realised it was a police car. The flashing lights came on and he signalled that I should stop by the side of the road. He had a forward-facing speed camera in the car, which seemed a little sneaky to me. I was then given a ticket which I had to take to a bank to pay the fine. Incidentally, if you're thinking about beating the cops at their own game by using a radar detector, be warned that they are illegal in many countries – including France and Spain – and you can be fined for just having one in the car, even if it's not switched on.

While I was handed the fine on the spot in New Zealand it's more likely these days that you might not even know you've been caught until you have returned home and the letter has been forwarded on from the car hire firm. Don't think you've got away with it if it's been a while, either. Our Mille Miglia trip was in September 2016. The notification of the fine came in the post – in a very spectacular envelope I will admit – in April of 2017.

Then there's Africa. My favourite story of speeding in Africa comes from a safari guide called Nate, who I met in South Africa. He had been driving in Zimbabwe, near Harare, when a cop stopped him for speeding, saying he had been caught by a radar further up the road. The policeman was close to the end of his shift, though, so rather than write out the ticket and demand the fine he asked to be driven to the local shebeen (bar) where he then told Nate to buy them both cheap beers for the rest of the evening.

My one experience of speeding in Zimbabwe also had a friendly outcome. I had only heard bad things about the Zimbabwean police – in my experience at least, quite wrong – and so was taking no chances. But then I was distracted, which is easy in Africa, and I must have crept over the speed limit just where a radar gun was pointed. A policeman then walked out into the middle of the road and signalled that we should pull over. He was with three others, but they remained sitting in the shade of a tree, chatting away. It must have been Joseph's turn.

I discovered his name was Joseph soon after the smiling cop issued me with the ticket. At first I had joked 'Will I go to prison?' which he thought was very funny, and after that we got on like a bush fire. He was very interested that in the UK you have to send your licence away to get points put on it for speeding. Here it was just paying $15 (US) in

▼ Cops are cops the world over, so be careful of your speed and always make sure you know the limits. *(Shutterstock)*

▼ A lot of effort goes into writing out a Tanzanian speeding ticket. *(Bresmedia)*

cash and getting a receipt. It had been such an entertaining conversation that I thought that maybe I should tip him, too.

I was also stopped for speeding in Tanzania. I'm still not sure I was actually speeding, but the policewoman showed me a picture of our car on her phone, and somehow that seemed to prove it. I suppose the point was that there was a radar at the place where the picture was taken.

The important things to remember are to always try to find out what the speed limit is and always be courteous if you're stopped. It's also advisable to stay in the car and keep your hands on the steering wheel. This is especially so in the United States, where the majority of police deaths are in just this sort of situation; which is why they might have their hand on the butt of their gun when they approach your car. If you are stopped, wind down the window, maybe put the interior light on if it's night-time and – it's worth repeating – keep both hands on the wheel, near the top where they can be seen. Don't get out of the car unless told to do so, and don't go rummaging around for your licence until you're asked to show it – the police officer might think you're going for a gun. Chances are cops in the States won't take you to a bar for a drink, but you never know.

Drinking and driving

On the subject of drinking, don't. Well, not if you're driving anyway. By all means have a beer or two or some wine in the evening – you're on holiday after all – but resist the temptation to have one with lunch, even if you're sure that will be within the legal limit. There's already enough to deal with driving in a foreign country, and it's simply not worth the risk.

There's another thing to think about, too. If you're a UK driver then you might be surprised to hear that England and Wales has one of the highest allowances for alcohol when driving in the world at 80 milligrams per 100 millilitres of blood. This means that while you might be okay with a small glass of wine or a swift half at home, the very same could take you over the limit elsewhere. You need to be careful how much you drink the night before, too. Alcohol is removed from the blood at the rate of about one unit every hour, though this does vary from person to person. But the best advice is to finish early and drink less.

If you do risk driving over the limit, then this might be sobering. In many countries drink driving can result in a prison sentence, especially if it leads to a fatal accident – and even the death penalty for one drunk driver in China after the crash he caused took the lives of four others.

Rules of the road

Other road laws will be different in foreign countries, too, and it's really up to you to keep on top of this and check out the rules of the road before you visit a country – the better

▲ If you're pulled over in the US – or anywhere else really – then keep your hands on the steering wheel where they can be seen. *(Ryan Fletcher / Shutterstock)*

▼ Drink driving is a sure way to ruin a road trip. *(Shutterstock)*

▼ Even in the middle of the Atacama Desert you will find police – though maybe they're not always very busy. *(Bresmedia)*

guidebooks are pretty good with this sort of thing. There's not the space here to go through all the laws in all the world, but just to show the variety – and at times absurdity – of some laws, here's a few of the best, or if you've been had up for any of them, worst.

In Estonia all cars must carry two wooden wheel chocks at all times; in Germany it's legal to drive your car while naked; in the US it's actually forbidden to drive an automobile while blindfolded (who knew?); while in Tennessee you're not allowed to shoot any animals from a car, except for whales (this is even more bizarre once you've looked for Tennessee on a map).

Of course, look into any of these in detail and they're usually archaic pieces of law that have just been left on the books, simply urban myths, or there might actually be a good reason for them – that could be the case with the blindfold thing, actually. But the point is, things are different in foreign countries, so don't expect the law to be the same as it is at home.

Accidents and emergencies

There are, of course, times when you might be glad to see a flashing blue, red or orange light, and that's when things go wrong, either for you or for fellow road users. In many countries you're required by law to stop at the scene of an accident. But you do need to use a bit of common sense; if there are a load of other people around and you don't speak the language then you can only get in the way, unless you have medical training.

If you're involved in an accident yourself, then you should make sure the police are called. The other party might not agree, but this is by far the most sensible course of action in

▲ It'll probably polish out… If the worst should happen then make sure you take notes and pictures; get as much detail as possible. *(Shutterstock)*

the majority of countries. You should also get hold of a copy of the police report; but before that make notes on the spot, lots of them, with as much detail as possible and, perhaps more importantly, take as many photographs as you can, too. Try to show the damage to the vehicle, any skid marks on the road, the deployed airbag, the number plates of the other cars involved and their positions at the scene of the crash. You also need to exchange insurance details and take the names, addresses and phone numbers of as many witnesses as possible. Oh, and whatever you do, never admit you're at fault, and never apologise, which amounts to the same thing.

▼ Even straight roads can catch you out, as the wrecks along the side of the road in northern Chile prove. *(Bresmedia)*

▲ A local garage in India will be able to fix just about anything, but especially tuk-tuks. *(Fotogenix / Shutterstock)*

▲ Even in the smallest of villages you will be able to find someone to help fix a puncture. *(Bresmedia)*

The next step is to contact your insurance provider as soon as possible to tell them about the accident. There is often a time limit on reporting accidents and if you wait too long before letting them know, you might find you're no longer covered.

If you have your accident in a hire car then you need to contact the car hire firm as soon as possible, too, while even the most innocuous of collisions need to be reported to the local police. And never get a car repaired without the approval of the hire company first.

Breakdowns

That last point goes for mechanical issues too, as the hire car firm will have its own breakdown cover and approved garages for fixing things. But if you're taking your own car and you're not a mechanic, or you don't have the tools, then it makes sense to extend your cover to include the countries you are visiting. If you're doing a single, long, road trip in a big country it might even be worth looking at joining a motoring organisation or taking out breakdown recovery insurance in that country.

Sometimes, though, if it's a more adventurous sort of trip, you will be on your own. And that can be all part of the fun. Some years ago, while in Turkey, I made a very temporary repair by lashing the exhaust up with the cord from a rucksack, though to be honest that's about the extent of my technical skills.

In many countries you will find people with the right skills quite easily, though. Often the car repair workshops will be lumped together in a cluster of banging, sizzling ingenuity on the edge of every town. In parts of Africa, South America and Asia you will find a mechanic who can fix just about everything – modern ECU and electrics etc. aside, perhaps.

Quite often, in many parts of Africa, you will be driving along and you will suddenly come across branches strewn,

▲ Warning triangles are mandatory equipment in many countries, while high-vis vests are in some, too. *(Shutterstock)*

seemingly willy-nilly, along the road. This is not the sign that an elephant has had a rushed breakfast – although I guess it could be – but rather that there's a broken-down or wrecked vehicle around the corner. In other parts of the world, and to be fair also in Africa, a warning triangle is used and very often carrying these is a legal requirement. You also need to use them. The last thing you want is to turn a drama into a tragedy by having a bus ploughing into your breakdown or minor shunt.

So, once you have parked in the safest place possible – off the side of the road if it's firm and clear and on a nice straight stretch if you can – put on the hazard lights and then place the triangle at least 45m (147ft) behind your broken-down vehicle, the UK's Highway Code advises. Then, of course, if you're as useless under a bonnet as I am, you will need to phone for help.

▲ **Smartphones have so many uses these days, including hosting handy navigation apps.** *(Shutterstock)*

▼ **If you *really* need to keep in touch with home then a satellite phone can be used just about anywhere.** *(Shutterstock)*

The first time I went travelling it was with a backpack and very little money, and in some places phoning home was close to impossible – I spent hours in a post office in Morocco one time in the 1980s trying to make a call to tell my folks I was still alive. These days, home is rarely far away, even if you're on the other side of the world. I'm not sure if that is actually a good thing. But it's the way it is. Much of the time, at least.

Being connected has its advantages, of course, particularly in the event of an emergency, and many people today, perhaps the vast majority in the developed world, would be lost – often quite literally – without their smartphones. In fact, these are now so much more than telephones that people can forget that that's what they actually are. But your smugly smart smartphone is just a useless oblong if it doesn't work – actually, they are still good for throwing; I throw mine quite often. So, if being connected is important to you then you will need to make sure your BingBong Artichoke 12 actually works in the country or countries you're visiting on your road trip, and you will also need to be aware of the parts of these countries – quite often the best bits – where it might not work.

The main thing to remember with your phone is to switch the roaming off. At the time of writing this wasn't an issue in Europe, as from the summer of 2017 mobile phone operating companies in the EU had to charge the same rates as you'd get at home. Further afield, though, the local network will charge your network for you watching cats play chess on the internet; and it gets expensive, especially as the phone – being oh-so-smart – will keep refreshing itself with hearty feasts of data. Much better to use a local sim card (make sure your phone is unlocked before you leave home); buy a bundle for travel from your own network provider or, best of all, make use of free Wi-Fi where and when you can.

Another useful tip, though not always practical, is to switch off the voicemail – you will need to ask your phone company to do this – as you can be charged for listening to your messages abroad, and these charges can be whopping. And perhaps most important of all, take your charger and make sure you have an adapter so you can actually plug it in.

If you're going well off the beaten track, more expedition than road trip, or if you simply *need* to be able to contact someone, then there are always satellite phones. These are no longer prohibitively expensive to buy, they can include Wi-Fi, and they can even be rented for the duration of your journey. We took one on a big African trip; never used it, but it was good to know it was there.

On the subject of phones, it's not illegal to use one when driving in every country, but just don't. Driving in a foreign land will often take much more concentration than driving at home, so if you need to make a call then stop somewhere safe to do so.

But using phones while at the wheel aside, there's actually a lot to be said for driving like a local. I find it happens quite naturally. It can be safer, too. Not just in terms of speed differentials on fast roads – perhaps more of a danger than speed itself – but also because it's less likely you will be taken for a tourist, which in some countries can be translated as 'target'.

Otherwise, driving is driving. But the things to remember when you're abroad is to always expect the unexpected – which isn't bad advice for home, actually – take plenty of breaks – which means you see more – and look far ahead. Try to read a situation in its prologue: a slow truck, a speeding car pulling out to overtake, a car parked a little way ahead of them, a blind brow… and ease off the gas.

Actually, easing off the gas – particularly when your car is loaded more than it usually is, which it could easily be on a road trip – is always good advice, as is braking progressively. Try to think about the way the weight transfers across your car; feel that happening when slowing and when in turns. Weight acts on the contact patches of your tyres, so when it comes off the rear when braking – and the same from the front when accelerating – it's easier to lose your purchase with the road at that end of the car. So get to know your car, and never stop getting to know your car.

Best of all, if it's a performance car or even a little warm, then take it on a track day, and sign up for some of the coaching that's invariably on offer at the better run events. What you will learn while sliding your car on a track could one day save your life; as the basic skills are transferable to other cars, of course, as any will slide in the right, or wrong, conditions. On top of that, a track day is also a great experience. Haynes has a book about all this, *The Track Day Manual*. I know the author quite well, but don't let that put you off.

Wildlife encounters

One often fun but potentially dangerous hazard you will encounter the world over is animals on the road. If it's a risk then you need to be ready for them, especially at night – it's one of the many reasons not to drive in the dark in some countries, as the tarmac holds in the day's warmth and so attracts critters of all types and sizes.

It's easy to think this is just about the developing world, but it's a hazard almost everywhere – you could encounter

▲ **Sometimes attitudes to road safety are different abroad – that's certainly the case in India.** *(Viikramaditya Rai / Shutterstock)*

▼ **The prospect of seeing wild animals on the road ahead is always exciting.** *(Bresmedia)*

▲ **Zebra crossing. You should always stop and let wild animals go first, and keep your speed down if there's a chance of an encounter.** *(Bresmedia)*

loose sheep and ponies on the Welsh and Scottish trips in this book, for example – and North America is certainly no exception. In Canada the etiquette is to slow down and alert other drivers by putting on your hazard warning lights. Elk and moose can get mesmerised by headlights in the night-time, and you really don't want to hit one of these, so go easy when it's dark

This is an approach that will work well anywhere; though you might want to dispense with the hazards if there's an elephant in the road, in which case it's about keeping your distance if you can and not making a sudden noise or movement, but also keep the engine running ready for a quick escape. An elephant *always* has right of way.

In Australia dawn and dusk are the most dangerous

times when it comes to kangaroos, but you should always be careful. Indeed, if you're driving in any part of the world where you know there's a good chance of an animal encounter, then go slowly; 50mph (80km/h) or less and much slower in a game park will not only give you the chance to react to a stray beast, but will also mean you've more chance of enjoying the sight of those other animals you may spot alongside the road.

If there is an animal in the way, then it's worth repeating, just stop and wait. Sometimes you might have to be patient; but remember, livestock apart, they were almost certainly there first.

Driving in the developing world

A quick word here on driving in Africa – but note that much of this is pertinent for most of the developing world. For all the reputation Africa has for danger, the chances are that the most hazardous thing you will do on an African road trip is the actual driving. Forget man-eating lions or Kalashnikov-toting bandits, it's the drunk driver that's the real mamba in the grass.

▼ **Driving in Africa and other developing parts of the world is great fun but you do need to keep your wits about you.** *(Bresmedia)*

This is just one of the reasons you should never drive at night – this is the same for many countries outside Africa too, and will crop up often in the following chapters – as is a lack of lights on cars, the general overuse of main beams, potholes and speed bumps that can be hard to spot and, as mentioned previously, animals on the road.

Also, bear in mind that some vehicles will not have mirrors, and even if they do they might not be used, and while – curiously – many Africans will drive at an unhurried pace, bus, taxi and minibus drivers always seem to be in a race – they often even have slick tyres!

You also need to be careful in small towns that see little traffic; children, dogs and chickens will run out without warning and if you hit anything it will be 100% your fault. Always. So take it easy in built-up areas, and always be ready for the unexpected.

But while that might sound a little daunting, it shouldn't put you off. The experience of driving in Africa is like nothing else and I've driven thousands of miles on this continent without a real problem, which means you can, too.

Off-roading

The African trips, more than most in this book, will be those where taking a 4x4 will probably be most advantageous, though that doesn't mean there will be serious off-road driving. But if there is a likelihood of serious off-roading on a trip you are planning then I would certainly recommend taking a course beforehand. Much of the driving I'd done before our big Africa trip had been performance based – racing in single seaters when I was younger, lots of track days since, and general hooning around for magazine car tests. But off-road driving is a completely different kettle of mud. The course we did was great fun, and very useful; it's good to know just how steep a bank you can traverse without toppling over. Surprising, too. This goes for bikes, too, only more so. Find a course and learn all you can before you set off on your trip. There is not the space to go into off-road driving and riding techniques in detail here, there are other books for both. But here are some points to think about.

Firstly, if there's an especially rough patch ahead then walk through it before you drive it, while another good tip is not to curl your thumbs round the rim of the steering wheel; hitting small rocks and ruts can cause the wheel to kick back and can break or bruise thumbs.

But the main thing is to let the truck do the work. When the going is very bad, put it in low range and let it crawl over the obstacles on the idle or with very little throttle. When the going's still rough but a bit quicker then don't force the car, coax it, let it flow, rather than manhandling it over the ground, which might cause damage. It's almost like being at the helm of a boat, if you get it right.

▼ Small minibuses like this are common across Africa, as is seeing one on its side (this is in Rwanda) or in a ditch. *(Bresmedia)*

It's rare that you will drive on sand, though it's possible in Namibia and on some other trips in this book if you choose to do so. The key thing is to reduce the tyre pressures to 1.5bar (21psi), which will give you a contact patch with a greater surface area. This is more practical in a properly equipped truck as they come with a compressor so you can pump the tyres up again – if you're in this sort of sand in a 2wd then you've probably taken a wrong turn, or you're at the beach.

Driving through soft sand is about momentum, trying not to use the brakes, and if you change gear making it quick and smooth. Mud, meanwhile, is about using low range and keeping the revs down; allowing the car to crawl through without wheelspin if you can. That said, sometimes you will need to take a more aggressive approach, just to get through, which is also a lot more fun.

▼ If you find yourself on a very rough section of road, you need to treat it with respect. *(Shutterstock)*

▲ **If you're forced to make a river crossing then make sure you check the depth first.** *(David Haykazyan / Shutterstock)*

Where's there's mud, there's water, and crossing rivers and water hazards needs care. First, make sure the 4wd and low range is selected – riverbanks can be steep and greasy and you will want to get out the other side. You also need to check the depth of the water – knee high is about the limit for an SUV, about waist high for a full-on 4wd, and look out for hidden hazards beneath the surface as you do so, but maybe check for crocodiles first!

Don't drive across if the water's flowing fast, for various reasons, not the least of which is the risk of being swept downstream, and also make sure you drive through very slowly, as you don't want water to surge and flood the sensitive bits of the car's electronics. Often a car or truck hire insurance will not cover water damage, so always err on the side of caution when it comes to literally dipping your headlights.

Rough stuff

Proper off-road driving and river crossings as described above are rarely a feature in the road trips in this book, and if there is a chance then that's mentioned in the Planning notes. But driving off the tarmac is a feature of a few of them; maybe even the best of them. And to be honest, even road trips that are designed to be fully paved will, in some countries, involve a little rough stuff, mainly because the best campsites, lodges or places of interest will be off the main road. In an ordinary car you just need to check beforehand that the road is not 4wd only – if it's leading to a hotel or a site of interest it probably won't be but with the former you

can check with a quick email or phone call. Some rough tracks are fine for 2wd, but you will need to take it slow.

In some countries the main roads can be gravel, and these can actually also be quite good, which can present its own problem for inexperienced drivers. Namibia is a good example of this, as the gravel roads here – on the whole – are excellent. This has meant that many people end up underestimating the amount of grip available while overestimating the amount of skill they possess. The word *many* in the sentence above is no exaggeration; a few years back one car hire company reported it had lost 10% of its Namibian fleet through single car accidents on gravel roads. This means that insurance excesses are high and, as mentioned above, sometimes the small print might even state that you're liable for all damage caused in a single car crash. The best advice is to keep below 50mph (80km/h) on gravel, and slow down some way before you think you need to when approaching a bend.

Corrugations

But whatever the risk, you will always take smooth gravel over corrugations. It's tempting to describe these as ripples in the road, but 'ripples' is such a gentle word, and 'corrugations' and 'gentle' should not be seen in the same sentence. Corrugations are formed along parts of the road where cars are continually slowing down or speeding up, after or before a rough patch or river crossing for instance, yet sometimes they can also go on for miles. Whatever advice you give for corrugations can be wrong.

You can take them very slowly, probably the safest and least damaging approach but hugely time consuming, or you can skim across the top of them at a fair speed, the car or

truck shaking like an old washing machine on spin cycle yet floating over the crests of the corrugations. The steering will be light, but it works, and it will certainly be less damaging than choosing an approach between these two extremes. You won't be going that fast really, but it will feel like 80mph. On ice.

All that said, there does often seem to be an optimum speed at which to drive over corrugations, at least when they're evenly spread, where a little slower and you'll be shaking out fillings and electrical connections, and a little faster and you could be close to losing control in an aquaplaning sort of way – let's call it *corruplaning*. But sometimes they are so uneven, or they are carpeting a rollercoaster of a road – which has caused them in the first place – that you just have to creep along; which is better than a duffed-up damper. At other times the nature of the corrugations can change while you're buzzing along them, causing an infernal shaking, and again only slowing right down will stop it.

After a while of driving on corrugations, even the keenest of 4x4 drivers might be glad to turn on to some silky smooth asphalt. Sometimes, though, you need to pay for the privilege when it comes to using the very best roads.

Paying your way

Toll roads are part and parcel of many motorway networks around the world. Tolls can be cheap, but they can also be very expensive, with Japan being very much in the latter category. Japan is also a good example of why they exist, too, as its expressways are the most astounding feats of engineering, and excellence comes at a price.

But it's the language barrier at the toll booth rather than the barrier across the road that's the real problem in Japan.

▲ Namibian gravel roads are usually in good condition – which brings its own dangers. *(Nick Fox / Shutterstock)*

▼ There's nothing more annoying to drive on than corrugations. This is a typical 'washboard' road in Australia. *(Shutterstock)*

▲ Automatic toll systems like the ETC in Japan are now common in many countries. *(Bresmedia)*

▼ An unusual petrol station in Shikoku, Japan; the hoses come down from above. Like many in Japan, this one was serviced. *(Bresmedia)*

Luckily, technology is good for stuff beyond smartphones and traction control and these days in most countries you are able to buy a card that fits in a box inside the car and this pays your way as you go, without you even having to stop – though you do usually have to slow down a bit. In Japan it's the ETC, and this can be arranged through the bigger hire car companies. This sort of technology makes a road trip easier, even if it does cut out yet another point of human contact – it used to be fun freaking out toll booth workers with a right hand drive car on the Continent with what appears to them to be a car without a steering wheel or even a driver.

Filling up

Similarly, filling up is getting more and more automated these days. You will still find that petrol stations are serviced in many countries, though, and if they are then one important tip is to make sure the pump is zeroed before they start to fill you up. This is a scam that's used the world over.

One important thing with fuel is being able to order what you want, so beyond the obvious of whether it's a diesel or petrol you need to know what these are in the language of the country you're driving in – it can be confusing. 'Petrol' will mean diesel in Cuba, for example.

In underdeveloped countries, when possible, it's worth going for the better known brands of fuel, too, as there can be issues with the quality. Also, with quite a few of the countries and trips featured in this book, fuel stations can be few and far between. The best advice in such a place is to always fill up when you can; sometimes even if you've only used a quarter of a tank. This will be repeated in many of the following chapters, simply because it keeps on being the very best advice.

The same is true if you're driving an EV, but when it comes to charging you really do need to plan your trip thoroughly in the first place. That does not just mean sussing out where the charging points along the way are, but also how you pay for them – the charge charge, if you like. This is an emerging market, and it is developing at a faster rate in different countries but, in essence, as far as payment is concerned then it's all as digital as you might expect, with a variety of network RFID cards and apps which will sometimes need to be pre-loaded with money before you hook up – regular credit/debit card payment is quite rare at the time of writing, though this will likely change.

The charging stations themselves tend to be in car parks, hotels and, of course, service stations, and come in two varieties: fast chargers or overnight. The latter is self-explanatory, you just plug it in and allow the battery to suck the electric from the grid (while not worrying too much where the grid gets its juice from, presumably) while the former is what we're after if we have a long day's drive. Tesla's

Supercharers are at the forefront of this technology, and its stations will have chargers in red – as opposed to its regular white – which will allow hook ups with cars with other types of connectors (yet another complication if you're planning an EV road trip). The fast charging stations will still take a bit of time, though, so it's best to factor in a lunch stop to coincide with your plugging-in time.

Finding these charging stations takes planning, but happily there is plenty of helpful advice available on the web – chargemap.com/map is a good place to start in Europe and there are similar resources the world over. At the time of writing there were over 150,000 charging stations spread across Europe – although this is by no means an even spread, with the Netherlands having 37,000 and Portugal 1,600 – and they tend to be unevenly spread on other continents, too.

It's clear to see why a phrase often associated with EV road trips is 'range anxiety'. But it's also easy to be negative about all this. Yet batteries, of course, have a positive terminal too, and in the lifetime of this book it's highly likely that an EV road trip will become as easy to plan as an internal combustion one.

I doubt plugging your car into a socket will ever be quite as memorable an experience as a fill-up in southern Africa, though, where a young lad or girl – and sometimes an old lad or old girl – will fill your car and almost always chat. I really enjoy these conversations, which are often very much a two-way discourse as believe it or not a foreigner like you and me is interesting. Yet they can go on for some time due to something which seems to be a peculiar thing to African filling stations: trying to get as much petrol in the tank as possible. Then a bit more.

▲ Stuarts Well Roadhouse on the Stuart Highway in Australia. It's important to fill up when you can on lonely roads. *(Sarena Hyland/Tourism NT)*

At home, when the mechanism clunks on the self-service pump its hand off the trigger, job done. Not so in Africa, that's just the start. Now the skill comes in, as they slowly dribble in fuel little by little, letting it settle before adding a bit more, like artists applying the final tiny tickle of a brush stroke to a masterpiece. I have sometimes wondered whether they are unaware that we do this ourselves at home and they believe we're in awe of the skill in which they control the pump trigger. Doesn't matter, it just stretches the always interesting or fun chat anyway. And sometimes a conversation at a petrol pump can result in good advice, too, even useful directions.

▼ Tesla's Supercharger stations are quicker than plugging your EV into the mains overnight, but they will still take a little while – try to coincide lunch stops with charging stops. *(Tesla)*

◀ **Our Japanese satnav, Yuka, shows us the way up the Irohazaka Winding Road.** *(Bresmedia)*

▶ **Always be aware that satnavs have their limits and have a backup means of navigation such as a road atlas or map to hand.** *(Shutterstock)*

Satnav

Why do I need a satnav when I have my own sat nag? That's what I used to say. The wife and I make a good team and Jassy's navigation skills are legendary, even if she does seem to have a problem with left and right at times. But Japan was different; we needed a belt and braces approach to this country, mainly because we did not know what to expect and we did not speak the language. In the end it was not a problem, our satnav, Yuka, worked perfectly – it's vitally important you give your satnav a name, otherwise it's difficult to shout at it, I mean her, without feeling stupid.

Well, actually, not quite perfectly. On the amazing elevated expressway through Osaka, Yuka kept telling us to turn sharp right, then left, when there was only a solid wall to turn in to, and then the city streets far below. It took us a little while to realise that those city streets below us were the problem. The GPS must have been seeing those rather than the expressway, and so was constantly trying to redirect us back on to the road we were actually on.

But it didn't matter too much as we'd strapped on our braces and done up our belts very tightly and there was no way we were going to find our navigational trousers around our ankles, because we had a map to hand, plus the Google Map directions printout in the road book and maps.me on the phone. We were then confident enough to ignore Yuka

▼ **A belt-and-braces approach can involve app, map and compass.** *(Bresmedia)*

for a while, and although she sulked a bit because she didn't like a brand new stretch of road between Himeji and Uji she did not let us down again.

Actually, this wasn't the first time we had used a satnav. We had also had one on our Mille Miglia trip, where it had been a great help in the Italian cities, and on our Tanzania and Chile trips. To be honest, the reason it took us so long to see the light was that we had always got along fine without them.

But there's another reason why you should not just rely on satnavs, though. These things are all about getting you from A to B as quickly as possible. They do not take local advice, and they do not possess common sense. A little while ago a woman was killed when her satnav directed her into a particularly nasty part of São Paulo. More prosaically both satnavs and maps.me have taken us on to awful roads in Africa that seemed like shortcuts to them, but ended up taking much longer to drive than the smoother way round. Use them, then, but use them in conjunction with guidebooks, maps and – often best of all – local advice.

Hiring satnavs for your hire car can also be expensive, though this is changing swiftly as these are supplied as part of the standard kit for many vehicles now and probably all cars in the coming years. But one way to beat the expense right now is to use your phone. Directions on Google Maps has served us well in the past, while the free apps HERE WeGo and maps.me are also good. Both of these let you download the maps while you're hooked up to Wi-Fi and then it's all in your phone ready to give you the directions as you drive when you're not connected, which is very useful.

Sign language

Whatever navigation method you use, you will still want and need to read road signs. In some countries this can be a challenge, when they are in Arabic, Cyrillic, Japanese or Chinese script. But on the main tourist routes you will be pleasantly surprised by how much Latin script and English language there is on road signs.

Warning signs and traffic notices can be different to what

▲ Even when signs are in Japanese you can often figure out what they're trying to tell you. *(Bresmedia)*

TOP 10
MOST CONFUSING EUROPEAN ROAD SIGNS

1. Alternative parking (no parking on the side of the number 1 on odd days and on the side of the number 2 on even days) Italy

2. Indirect left turn Italy

3. No vehicles carrying water pollutants Switzerland / Portugal

4. If you want to turn left from a main road then turn right first and take the road shown to cross the main road Spain

5. Priority on Turn France

6. Skiers allowed to cross road during these hours Germany

7. No handcarts or wheelbarrows France / Portugal

8. No Parking on verges / shoulder Germany

9. Accident ahead that's blocking the road France

10. Emergency lane with gravel pit Switzerland

▲ The top 10 most confusing European road signs.

(Easy Jet and Europcar / Quentin Devine)

you are used to at home, so although many of these are just common sense, it's worth brushing up on them if you can – often there will be an info sheet with this kind of thing that comes with the hire car; you know, that one you never realise is there until you drop off the car at the end of the trip? But for some really confusing road signs, just take a look at the top ten on the graphic on this page.

Of course, however confusing a sign is, in the final analysis, they are there to keep us safe. And, as we're always being told, safety is important.

Safety first

Foreign travel, and even driving abroad, is in most places a relatively safe pursuit. But there's one thing that wasn't an issue when I was younger – a good job too as I would never have got anywhere – and that's whether or not you should pick up hitchhikers. Most will say you shouldn't these days, but sometimes it would be churlish not to give someone a lift. It's a decision that you need to take in the where and the when, and it will depend largely on the country you're travelling in. But if you have the slightest doubt about giving someone a lift, then don't.

One other tip, regarding safety and security, is to carry a dummy wallet if you know there's an issue with crime in the country you're in. Put about £30 worth of sacrificial cash in it and some old out of date credit and debit cards. If you're robbed – which you almost certainly won't be – you can give them the decoy wallet. Everybody's happy… Well, for a little while at least.

Are we there yet?

When I was a lad, my brother and I used to travel down to Cornwall in the back of a Morris Marina estate with the dog and no air con in crawling traffic on country roads, with nothing to do other than than look out the window. But these days, kids need to be entertained. There is plenty of stuff on this on the internet – an astounding amount in fact. But the best advice I could pick out was fully loaded electronic devices, sick bags, snacks, lots of water and something called a scavenger hunt, where you need to spot things from a list; black dog, roadkill, orange car, wheelbarrow, MH370, and so on. Or maybe more fun for older kids, like me, makes of car. There are many of these that are printable on the web.

It's up to you whether you take your children on your road trip. It could be a great experience for them, or they might be bored out of their minds. Only you will know that, and I guess it largely depends on their age. But if you do take them, then you might want to devise a route with easy stages and plenty of stops.

Talking of childish things, it's sometimes nice to have something to make a car your own, even if it is a hire car, and a mascot is great for this. We have Horsey-Giraffe, who sits on the dashboard, always looking strangely superior, even regal. But then he is probably the most widely travelled little giraffe who looks a bit like a horse in the world. So, then, Horsey-Giraffe; where next?

Chapter 2

EUROPE

From sinuous Alpine passes to
unrestricted autobahns, or coastal
roads clinging to jagged shorelines
to byways that have been used
since the time of the Romans,
Europe has plenty to offer when
it comes to driving experiences.
Throw in easy border crossings and
a change in culture every couple
of hundred miles and you have the
perfect recipe for road trip success.
The only real problem is deciding
which one to drive first…

◀ Car negotiating the Julier Pass in the Swiss Alps.
(Shutterstock)

What better for a European road trip than one that celebrates speed, the automobile and the art of performance driving while visiting seven different countries?

It might not be the first choice for everyone (Eurotunnel's Le Shuttle is certainly quicker) but there is something to be said for starting your European road trip – if you're coming from the UK – by ferry. Crossing the English Channel has marked the beginning of adventures for centuries, and there's still a certain romance when you gaze back at the ever-diminishing seam of the White Cliffs of Dover, while you look forward to the days on the road ahead of you.

And for this particular trip there was plenty to anticipate. The plan was to visit seven countries in eight days in the MX-5 we then had. But the main objective was to drive some of the greatest Alpine passes, max out the car on the autobahn, get in a little track time, and visit some of motorsport's holy places – as well as some motoring museums that must rank as among the very best in the world. One for the car lover this then, but mostly one for the driver.

▼ The old Reims grand prix circuit is the ideal place for a pit stop on a European road trip. *(Bresmedia)*

To get anywhere from Calais there's usually a bit of motorway driving to do, but you should be in Reims in under three hours. This is often the first stop for any self-respecting race fan, because outside this interesting cathedral city (turn off the A26 and onto the N31 then turn left towards Gueux) lie the remains of the old grand prix venue, used for Formula 1 until 1966. The tribunes, pits, timing box and some of the other furniture of this road circuit are still just sitting there, a lost temple to speed. It's been refurbished, so it's not quite as evocative as it was a few years back, but it's a great place to stop for a picnic lunch and to get some shots of your car parked up where Tazio Nuvolari, Juan Manuel Fangio, Jim Clark and many other greats from motor racing's history once made their pit stops.

The track is mostly still there, too, and with the use of an old map (easy to find on the net) it's possible to trace it. This was a high-speed circuit in days gone by, known for close slipstreaming action. It was also dangerous. I don't believe

▶ **The Cité de l'Automobile National Museum in Mulhouse houses the largest car collection in the world.**
(Jef Wodniack / Shutterstock)

in ghosts, but when the wind blows through the grandstand there's a certain atmosphere at Reims…

There was more history at our next stop, Mulhouse, home of the Cité de l'Automobile, the French national motor museum, which is based around the Schlumpf Collection – said to be the largest display of rare automobiles in the world, including a fair few old Bugattis.

From Mulhouse it was on to Switzerland and the start of the proper driving with the passes. The first pass of note we hit was the Flüela (approached from near Davos). I should point out here that this wasn't at the busiest time, but in September; not so late that the snow had fallen to close the passes yet late enough that France and Italy had gone back to work and school. But what was particularly memorable about Flüela, which has a series of hairpins and some more flowing corners too, was that it was sunny and we had the roof down, yet at the top there was snow all around us. A lovely experience, that.

There are many Swiss Alpine passes to consider; you could easily take a fortnight and more just ticking them off. A few favourites include the Klausen Pass, the Gotthard, the Furka (which starred in the *Goldfinger* James Bond film), Grimsel, and Susten, each of which is a challenging and fun drive.

But one thing about passes is that the roads to and from them – which is the bit you're interested in – are up or down, and they can be steep. If you have a rear-wheel drive car then a lot of the fun is going up, steering a little with the throttle when you can (when the way is clear), but whatever car you're in you need to keep an eye on your brakes. Race tracks aside there's nothing quite as punishing for pads as coming off a pass.

We headed for the Stelvio Pass next, a great drive in itself, which included the Umbrail Pass – now fully paved. Stelvio is perhaps the best known of all the Alpine passes, and this means it's often cluttered with cyclists and campervans, but it's still an experience worth having – just try to get on it early in the morning and note that while the 48 hairpins of its northern approach are more famous, the road on the Italian side is probably the more enjoyable drive.

◥ **The Italian side of the Stelvio Pass.** *(Bresmedia)*

▶ **An MX-5 is great fun on an Alpine pass – I'm not missing the apex, I'm missing a cyclist!** *(Bresmedia)*

▲ There's not much that can beat the Grossglockner High Alpine Road when it comes to driving experiences. *(Bresmedia)*

Many will actually say Stelvio is on their bucket list, but for me Grossglockner in Austria was always the one. This is because it's associated with a motor racing era I've always been particularly fascinated in, a time when the Nazi-backed teams of Mercedes and Auto Union dominated grand prix racing in the 1930s. But hillclimbing was also big news back then, and the daddy of all 'mountain races' was Grossglockner.

▼ The weather closing in on a section of the Grossglockner. *(Bresmedia)*

It was actually quite a drive east to get to the Grossglockner High Alpine Road, yet it was good stuff most of the way. The road is named for the mountain it skirts, at 3,798m (12,461ft) the highest in Austria (we're in country number five now, having popped into Lichtenstein for lunch, and then dipped into Bormio in Italy from the Stelvio Pass to spend a night).

The pass itself does not disappoint in terms of a scenic route and certainly in terms of a driving challenge, with far more flowing curves than many of the other passes and some places – tourist traffic allowing – where you can really get up to speed. Some of the corners had meltwater flowing across them in little streams, which certainly added to the adventure. Years ago it was all adventure, as the whole way was paved with cobbles, which must have been interesting in a 600bhp Auto Union, but now it's smooth tarmac – though you can take the spur road to Edelweisspitze just before the top to get a flavour for how it once was, plus a view that will drop your jaw some 2,564m (8,400ft).

Coming off the pass we stayed in Zell am Zee, which in keeping with the theme of this trip is the location of the Porsche family's farm and Ferdinand Porsche's base, along with his design office, during the war. It's a lovely town, set on a lake – just the place to design tanks for the Nazis… What, you didn't know?

The next day it was raining pretty hard when we crossed into Germany from Austria, and then the first taste of the autobahn was a huge traffic jam – when all's said and done they're still motorways and even if it's okay to go as fast as you like, as fast as you like is as slow as the car in front if you can't get by.

It was actually traffic all the way to Munich on this particular day. This city is worth a visit just for the bierkellers – I love the Hofbräuhaus for its folksy fun – and the wurst, but in the spirit of this trip there's also the Deutsches Museum, housed in a fantastic old building on an island in the Iser. The main museum is great, but for cars, motorcycles and other transport go to Deutsches Museum Verkehrszentrum.

On leaving Munich we hit our first stretch of unrestricted and uncongested autobahn. Now the thing about going fast is that you get to the scene of the accident – which is not necessarily your accident to begin with – very quickly. So you need to be very careful on the autobahns; and always try to make smooth and steady applications on the wheel and the pedals.

The sign for an unrestricted section of autobahn is the same as for national speed limit applies signs in many countries, a diagonal slash, but if there is no limit indicated then this also means just that: no limit. There's an important thing to remember here, though: just because the sign says there are no restrictions, it's not a licence for lunacy. This is a rough translation from the German version of the Highway Code: 'Any person driving a vehicle may only drive so fast that the car is under control. Speeds must be adapted to the road, traffic, visibility and weather conditions as well as the personal skills and characteristics of the vehicle and load.' So you always have to drive to the prevailing conditions, in terms of the density of traffic and the weather, and always within your car's limits, and your limits.

But when the weather's nice, and the road is clear, driving at high speed is one of the great thrills of life – and

▲ **Autobahns are not dead straight and you will even find unrestricted sections with curves.** *(Shutterstock)*

one you can't take for granted, as there's always rumours that Germany will one day set a speed limit across its autobahn network. At the time of writing, about two-thirds of these motorways are unrestricted, though there's often an advisory top speed displayed and limits can sometimes be applied when the weather's bad and always when there are roadworks.

▼ **A Porsche 917 KH in the Porsche Museum, Stuttgart – you'd be hard pressed to find a better sculpture at the Louvre.** *(Roman Belogorodov / Shutterstock)*

▲ **What better way to finish off a European road trip than with a few hot laps around the Nürburgring?**
(Frozenspeed Motorsport Photography)

One rather marvellous stretch of autobahn was between Stuttgart and Speyer on this particular trip. Or to put it another way, between the home of Mercedes and Porsche and the Hockenheim race track. Both German manufacturers are very proud of their heritage and each has an excellent museum in Stuttgart. It's hard to say which is better; but one has a Mercedes W125; then again the other has a Porsche 917. Visit both.

Hockenheim is also interesting. Although for many years it was seen as the poor relation to the mighty Nürburgring, it has a history – and for many years a character – all of its own. It used to be all about flat-out blasts through the forest, then a twiddly stadium section in an arena. I always used to enjoy it as a grand prix venue, but sadly it fell victim to the homogenisation of F1 circuits, becoming another bent paper clip of a race track. It now has a great motorsport museum which not only boasts a few F1 cars but also the largest collection of racing motorbikes in Europe.

We left the charming town of Speyer, which is near Hockenheim, very early the next day, a sunny September Sunday. There was no one on the autobahn, except for one guy in an old Ferrari 308 GTB, but before I could say 'Kraftfahrzeughaftpflichtversicherung' he was gone (in case you were wondering, that means 'automobile liability insurance'). Now an MX-5 is not the fastest thing in the world, but it was fast enough, and on the section of autobahn from Speyer heading in the direction of Trier, which even had some long sweeping curves, the driving was thoroughly engrossing – though I couldn't help wondering what it would have been like in that Ferrari.

But curves on an autobahn are one thing, curves on the 'Ring are another thing altogether. If you're only a little interested in cars and driving then you will know that for a few euros you can take your own car out on to the Nordschleife of the Nürburgring. It's an amazing experience, if a little daunting first time. The best advice is to treat it as a fast road drive to begin with, and always keep an eye on your mirrors. Oh, and check it's open to 'tourist traffic' on the day you want to visit, as often it's booked up by car manufacturers, while it's still used for racing, too. So do your research before visiting the 'Ring, and note that there is a real risk that if you crash you can face a big bill for fixing barriers and the like.

It's fun to stay the night at the Nürburgring, too, the bars and restaurants have racing themes and there will be plenty of people with whom you can shoot the line about your epic high-speed European road trip. Oh, and don't forget to pop into Spa-Francorchamps on the way back to Calais through Belgium, if only to take a look at just how steep the climb up from Eau Rouge really is, while the 100km drive there from the 'Ring is pretty good, too.

Seven countries (you could make it eight by popping into Luxembourg), eight days, 1,740 miles (2,800km), plus four legendary race circuits, three of the world's greatest car museums, as many Alpine passes as you can squeeze into the time you have, and as much top speed as your car can manage. It all adds up to one amazing road trip.

PLANNING NOTES

Start and finish: Calais.
Distance: 1,740 miles (2,800km).
Time needed: Around eight days to do it all; though you could spend an extra week or so exploring the Alpine passes.
When to go: The passes close in winter and sometimes only open late in spring – the high ones in June – and can close early in autumn, so check this before setting out.
Vehicle: There's nothing like a small rear-wheel drive sportscar for tackling the passes; but then there's nothing like a supercar for the autobahn. Decisions, decisions…

Beware of: Drive to the conditions on the autobahn and be aware that people in front of you might not be able to judge just how fast you're approaching.
Detours, extensions and variations: As well as ticking off the passes there's also all of Italy to play with, or why not try out the great driving roads in Germany's Black Forest, which is close to this route?
Further information: Check out nurburgring.org.uk for all things to do with the 'Ring while www.myswissalps.com/car/trafficinfo is good for info on whether the Swiss passes are open or closed.

▲ **Better known as the Ring Road, Route 1 runs right around Iceland.** *(Shutterstock)*

Just the name seems otherworldly; a land of ice. But Iceland, while it does have gargantuan glaciers to ogle, is also about the heat from the core of the earth itself, which means volcanoes, hot springs, glooping mud pools, geysers and lava fields. Oh, and there's also a rather good road trip to be had there.

The best of Iceland, arguably, can be seen in one glorious 830 mile (1,330km) drive, called the Ring Road, or more formally Route 1. You can start at the capital Reykjavik or the main airport Keflavik, 30 miles (48km) away – which is close to the famous Blue Lagoon spa – then, heading anti-clockwise, the first site is the Seljalandsfoss falls and then the staggering 60m (196ft) falls at Skógafoss. But before all this it's worth driving the Golden Circle, which is a well-known tourist route that can be completed in a day, encompassing some of Iceland's most iconic natural and historical sites, including Geysir – with spectacular hot water spouts from which all other geysers get their name – Gullfoss falls and Thingvellir National Park.

Back on the Ring Road, from Skógafoss it's on to Vik – a quiet town with wide volcanic black beaches and surreal basalt rock formations – then the wonderful wilderness of Skaftafell, before driving on to Jökulsárlón. The inlet the road bridge crosses here leads to a glacier lagoon that is full of icebergs all year long, some of them a luminous blue. It's a great place for a boat trip and a popular hangout for seals. Höfn is next, a good base from which to set off on trips to the immense Vatnajökull glacier, which covers much of the south-eastern part of Iceland.

The Ring Road then twists up the east coast, before it cuts inland to Mývatn, a magical volcanic area with vibrant colours, hot springs and a spectacular crater lake. Mývatn advertises itself as the 'Northern Lights capital

◀ **The 60m falls at Skógafoss – typical of the dramatic scenery this true land of fire and ice has to offer.** *(Promote Iceland)*

of Iceland' but on the downside the name translates as 'Midge Lake', and there are clouds of the pesky things in the summer.

From Mývatn it's not so far to drive to the charming city of Akureyri, known as the capital of the north and home to the world's most northerly golf course, which holds a summer tournament under the midnight sun.

The route then goes via historic Borgarnes to complete the loop at the quirky capital of Reykjavik, an interesting place in itself with fine dining, excellent museums and great nightlife.

PLANNING NOTES

Start and finish: Reykjavik.
Distance: 830 miles (1,330km).
Time needed: Eight to ten days, including a day in Reykjavik, should be sufficient.
When to go: Summer is the obvious time, but then that's also the busiest, and despite the island being mostly wilderness and very sparsely populated you might have to put up with big crowds and traffic at the more popular sites, so the shoulder seasons (May and September) should not be discounted. Winters are cold and you won't see much daylight.
Vehicle: If you're going in the high season then make sure you book a hire car early. A 2wd car is fine for the Ring Road, but if you're looking at taking some detours off the main route, or if you're going in the autumn or winter, then 4wd is recommended. Be warned, car hire is expensive in Iceland.

Beware of: If you're travelling in summer be sure to book ahead for accommodation and activities. Watch out for speed traps all along the Ring Road, especially around Akureyri, as fines are steep. Also, while not as cold as you might think, it is 'Iceland' – winters are bitter, and even in summer the weather can be unpredictable, so pack for wind and rain.
Detours, extensions and variations: Add a day to drive the Golden Circle.

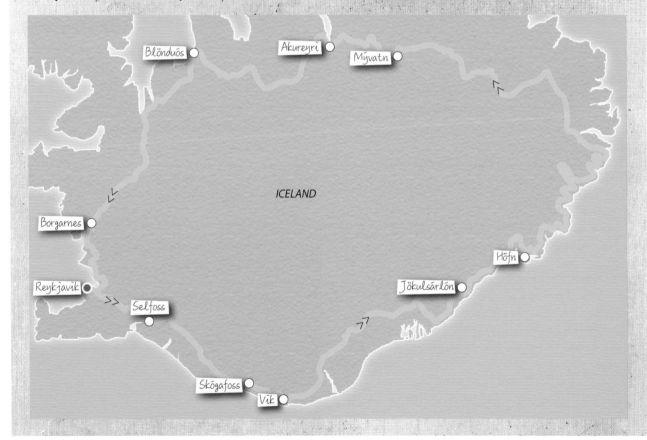

ICELAND

Blönduós
Akureyri
Mývatn
Borgarnes
Höfn
Reykjavik
Jökulsárlón
Selfoss
Skógafoss
Vík

◀ Stirling Moss took just over ten hours to complete the 1,000 mile (1,609km) Mille Miglia route in 1955 in a Mercedes 300 SLR, but it also makes for a great week-long road trip. *(Mercedes-Benz)*

east. A little further out of Brescia, though, on the old route, the excellent Museo Mille Miglia (on Viale della Bornata) will give you a wonderful feel for the race you're about to retrace.

Much of the route from there, rather wonderfully, takes in many of Italy's best sights. First off is Lake Garda, then Verona, then Padua and Ravenna – it's also not far off the route to visit San Marino. From here it was once a blast down the coast, touching 170mph (273km/h) and more in the big cars, but it's much slower going now and to be honest it makes more sense to use the autostrada most of the way to Pescara.

From Pescara it's into the Apennines and some very good driving roads – look out for a preserved section of old Mille Miglia road surface on a hairpin as you descend into Antrodoco, which will give you a great insight into how it was in the 1950s.

Rome is Rome, of course, and then there's the Via Cassia to Viterbo (a wonderful road with plenty to see) before you head north to Sienna and Florence; with the beautifully flowing Radicofani pass along the way. But the passes that really made the Mille Miglia were the Futa and the Raticosa; the first close to an Alpine pass with its crinkle of hairpins at the top, the next – they are joined by a saddle – more fluid and fast.

After Bologna it's an obligatory detour to Maranello, the home of Ferrari, before it's back to Brescia via Piacenza and Mantua. One thousand miles, many thousand memories.

▼ There's not much to mark the old route, but we did find this plaque at the top of the Futa Pass. *(Bresmedia)*

In 1955 Stirling Moss, guided by the fearless Denis Jenkinson, won the Mille Miglia in a time of 10 hours, 7 minutes and 48 seconds – that's an average speed of 99mph (160km/h). Which, when you consider the 1,000 mile (1,609km) route included mountain passes and blasts through tight medieval cities, is pretty good going.

We followed the same route over 60 years later and it took us seven days. That said, we were in no rush, and rather than a 310bhp Mercedes 300 SLR we had a 60bhp Lancia Ypsilon hire car at our disposal. Oh, and I'm not Stirling Moss…

The Mille Miglia was one of the biggest races on the sportscar calendar. It ran from 1927 to 1957, before it was stopped after an accident in which nine spectators were killed. It used a number of routes over the years but we opted for the classic configuration used from 1954 to 1957. Because it's a loop you need not begin at Brescia, as the race did, and we picked up our car at Rome. But Brescia's a great city, so let's be like Moss and start there.

Concentrating on the Mille Miglia sites (though there's much more to the city) the smart marble-lined Piazza della Vittoria, where the cars were scrutineered, is easy to find but there's nothing to mark where the start ramp was – this was where the short Viale Rebuffone meets Viale Venezia to the

PLANNING NOTES

Start and finish: Brescia (or any city along the way).
Distance: 1,000 miles (1,609km).
Time needed: Bear in mind this route includes some of the great Italian cities and you could take a very long time over it, but a week is fine if you're mainly interested in the drive.
When to go: In the height of summer the tourist sites are rammed – Florence was very busy even when we went in September – so the shoulder seasons are best. The race was usually at the end of April or beginning of May.
Vehicle: This is the perfect trip for a classic; but a hire car will do.

Beware of: Watch out for overzealous police. The route is quite easy to follow, as it's the old main roads, but you'll need to research it. There are maps of the old route on the internet.
Detours, extensions and variations: You're going through Pescara anyway, so it would be rude not to trace the old 16 mile (25km) grand prix circuit, which loops through Case Frascone, Spoltore and Cappelle Sul Tavo before spearing back down towards the coast through Montesilvano, then turning right to pass through Pescara itself along Via Adriatica.

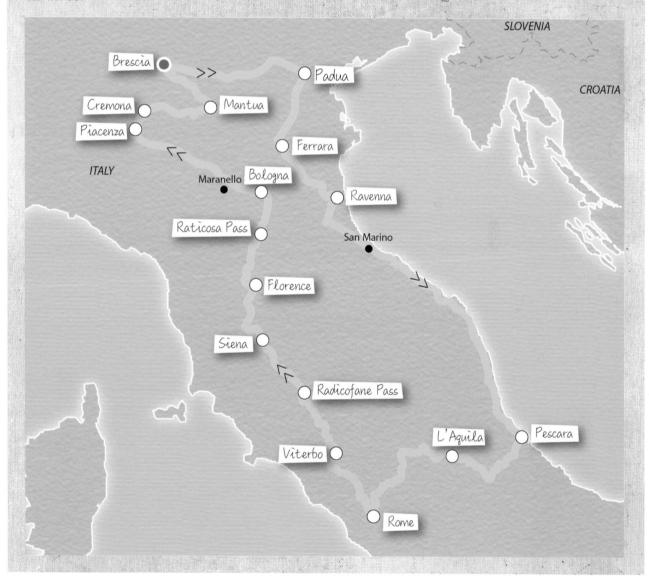

What is it about an island that makes you want to drive around the edge of it? Maybe it's something entangled in our DNA, the way our ancient ancestors used to travel, skirting the coast? I'm not sure about that, but it's certainly a good way to see Sicily.

Assuming you're coming in by air, though there are also ferries from mainland Italy, then a good starting point would be Catania, but the beauty of a loop is that you can, of course, start anywhere along it. It's a journey through time this one, so it seems right to go in the direction of the clock, heading south to Syracuse – once the home to Archimedes and now a UNESCO World Heritage site. From Syracuse head north-west via Noto (exuberant baroque architecture and scrumptious ice cream) to one of the highlights of the trip, Agrigento's Valley of the Temples with its gorgeous ancient Greek ruins.

Heading up the coast it's then worth fitting in a drive along the ancient saltpans that stretch from Marsala to Trapani; with its lagoons, windmills and mounds of salt it's certainly different. And then there's the ancient city of Segesta and the hill town of Monreale (don't miss the duomo) on the way to the island's capital, Palermo; frenetic and interesting, but bypass it if it's not for you.

Driving east along the north coast you can stop off at picturesque Cefalú, with its long sandy beach, before cutting

▲ **Road trips in Sicily are trips back in time. Here a massive sculpture of Icarus lies in front of the Concordia Temple in the Valley of Temples in Agrigento.** *(Leo Salas Z / Shutterstock)*

the corner and taking the SS185 through the Peloritani Mountains from Tonnarella to Taormina, the latter with its ancient theatre which offers stunning views of Etna. There's something so deliciously menacing about an active volcano, smoking away in the background to remind you of the fire within. But make sure you get close to the volcano, too, as it's an amazing experience – when we visited I was particularly struck by the walls of solidified lava that blocked some of the roads.

But while Etna was quite literally awesome, we will need to rewind a few miles for my personal highlight. The Targa Florio was one of the last great road races, held from 1906 until the 1970s. At the end of its time, pukka Le Mans-style

▼ **The scenery and roads on the Targa Florio route have not changed much, though you won't see a Ferrari 512 S these days – this is in 1970.** *(Rainer Schlegelmilch / Motorsport Images)*

racing cars blasted along these twisting roads and through the streets of the small country towns. But you will only appreciate just how insane this really was by driving the route yourself. The Piccolo Madonie course, as it was called, is about 31 miles (50km) east of Palermo. Head for the start at Cerda, and the now disused pit buildings. There's plenty on the web on how to follow this, but basically you link Cerda with Caltavuturo, Collesano then Campofelice, and then what used to be a flat-out blast parallel to the coast before turning back towards Cerda to complete the 44 mile (71km) lap.

PLANNING NOTES

Start and finish: Catania.

Distance: 560 miles (900km).

Time needed: There's certainly enough to see and do to justify ten days to a fortnight, but you could do this in a week at a push.

When to go: It gets very hot and crowded in the summer and spring is a perfect time to visit Sicily.

Vehicle: The main roads are pretty good, so a hire car will do fine. One thing, if you have a supercar then think twice about taking it on the Targa Florio course, it really is in quite poor condition with the road surface crumbling in places last time I drove it.

Beware of: I've seen people texting while driving a number of times, but only in Sicily did I see a girl texting on *two* phones, steering with her knees... on the motorway. Driving in Sicily is about making sure everyone else knows where you're going, which means using the horn as much as the indicators. It's an experience, though.

Detours, extensions and variations: Shorten the loop and heighten the driving experience by heading north from Agrigento to Palermo along the SS118 via Corleone.

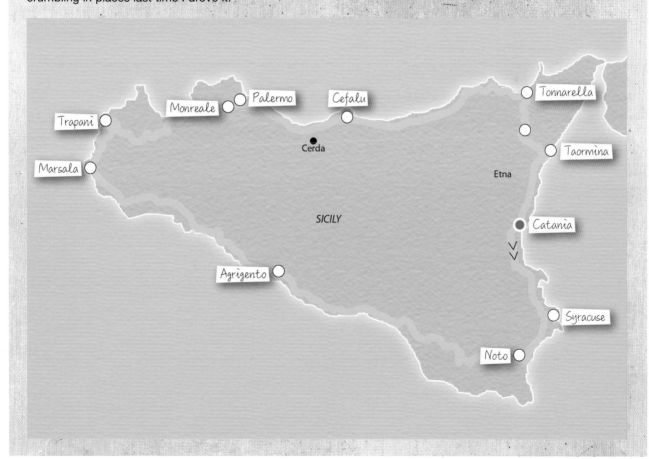

The North Coast 500 might sound like a NASCAR race, but it's actually the name given to what's promoted as 'Scotland's answer to Route 66'. That too is a little misleading, as the NC500 is not really anything like the American classic. In fact, in some ways it's better, as this coastal loop ticks off everything that makes a Scottish road trip one to savour, including rugged mountains, atmospheric ruins and remote beaches – not to mention some very fine driving roads.

The route is actually 516 miles in all, starting in Inverness and then heading to the west coast at Applecross, wending its way up to Torridon and Ullapool before hitting the far north of the land at Caithness and John o'Groats, then heading back south to Inverness to complete the loop.

For such a remote part of the country there's a remarkable amount of things to see and do along the NC500 and highlights include the crumbling ruins of Ardvreck Castle on the edge of Loch Assynt; pristine and secluded Balnakeil beach in Sutherland; the amazing Smoo Cave (also in Sutherland); John o'Groats (close to the most northerly point on the UK mainland): Dunrobin Castle, a French-style chateau just south of Brora; and more mountain hikes than you could shake a walking pole at.

As far as driving is concerned it's all memorable, but a standout section is the hairpin-riven 626m (2,053ft) ascent up the winding Bealach na Bà (or Applecross Pass) between Kishorn and Applecross, which is both steep (hitting gradients of 20% in places) and spectacular.

With all the above in mind it's no surprise that these roads are busier than they were before the NC500 was contrived – this was only in 2015 so it's a remarkable success story – but it's still an amazing drive. Yet maybe the best advice is to do it before it becomes *too* popular.

▲ **A motorcyclist riding the North Coast 500 passes the ruins of Calda House and Ardvreck Castle on Loch Assynt.** *(Shutterstock)*

▼ **The most challenging driving on the North Coast 500 is to be found on Bealach na Bà, also known as the Applecross Pass.** *(Shutterstock)*

PLANNING NOTES

Start and finish: Inverness.
Distance: 516 miles (830km).
Time needed: Five to seven days is recommended.
When to go: Between May and September is the most popular time but autumn and winter are doable, although some attractions close in the winter months.
Vehicle: There are hire car options in Inverness, including companies that offer classics and supercars.
Beware of: The NC500 has been a marketing success story, but a surge in demand means you might want to book ahead for accommodation. Single-track roads and wandering sheep bring their own hazards and note that the Bealach na Bà is not suitable for motorhomes and caravans, but there is an alternative route.
Detours, extensions and variations: If you're using your own car you'll need to get to Inverness in the first place so why not make this into a sort of figure-of-eight by connecting Edinburgh; Fort William; Loch Ness (then do the NC500) then south from Inverness via Pitlochry? This takes in some excellent roads.
Further info: www.northcoast500.com

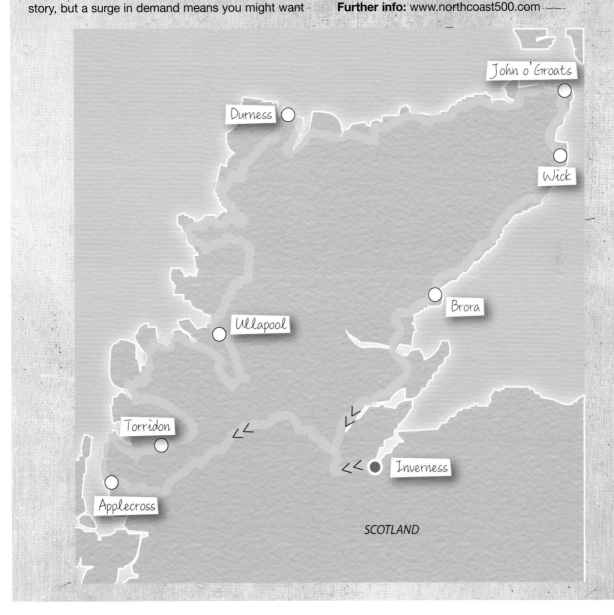

John o'Groats

Durness

Wick

Brora

Ullapool

Torridon

Inverness

Applecross

SCOTLAND

▲ A motorcyclist powers up to the Vršič Pass in the Julian Alps in Slovenia. *(Shutterstock)*

The very best road trips can be journeys with a purpose. For instance, we went to the Balkans on a research trip for a novel, but we left with an excellent road trip under our belt.

It all started in Zagreb (Croatia), a fascinating city, but the really interesting thing about this trip was crossing the borders, as this is one of the few places in Europe in which you can add to your passport's stamp collection. Crossing into Bosnia, the change was simply remarkable. It really was a different land altogether with its pen-like minarets and more *inshallah* attitude to driving. This wasn't so very long after the end of the Bosnian war, really, a decade and a bit, and reminders of it were common. In Bihać some of the buildings still bore the scars from automatic weapons, and when you see what they can do to stone and concrete it turns your stomach a little to think about what effect they have on flesh and bones. There's much more to Bihać than that, though; the lovely Una National Park is close by, for a start. We wished we had stayed longer in Bosnia.

As it was we were soon heading back into Croatia, stopping off at the extraordinary Plitvice Lakes National Park, a quite magical place where you can walk down a completely natural terrace of cascading lakes, almost each and every one a different colour, ranging from green to blue, to an aquamarine shade and even grey. Chameleon-like, these are constantly changing, depending on how the sunlight hits them and the quantities of various minerals slushing through the water. From there the road to the coast is a cracker, then the drive up to Istria along the Adriatic Highway is both beautiful and interesting.

We spent some beach time on the Istrian Peninsula before heading north to Slovenia; and some wonderful driving roads all the way to Bovec, and the amazing turquoise waters of the Soca River – the area is both spectacular and fascinating, especially if you have an interest in the First World War, while it's also great for kayaking and hiking.

After that we headed north over the Julian Alps via the Vršič Pass (1,611m or 5,285ft), a fantastic road with 50 hairpins, some of which are cobbled. From there it was back to Zagreb via Lake Bled, with its picturesque island and clifftop castle, and Ljubljana.

For this trip's map I've included Mostar in Bosnia (famous for its arched bridge), then up to Plitvice via the coast, as this is what we wished we had done at the end of it – that's one sad thing about many road trips, there's never quite the time to see it all, nor drive it all.

▼ The Plitvice National Park in Croatia is quite simply astonishing. *(Shutterstock)*

PLANNING NOTES

Start and finish: Zagreb.

Distance: 1,030 miles (1,660km) including the extension shown on the map.

Time needed: Ten days to two weeks would work, including a few days soaking up the sun on the coast.

When to go: We did this trip in October and it was perfect, with nice autumn sunshine and no crowds in the tourist traps like Plitvica.

Vehicle: Hire car from Zagreb; the roads were generally good everywhere.

Beware of: Much of former Yugoslavia was sown with landmines during the 1990s conflict and while there's a lot of talk that Bosnia in particular has yet to be cleared, the risk is very small; but to make sure there's no risk whatsoever stick to marked hiking trails and roads. Note that the Vršič Pass is only open from May to October.

Detours, extensions and variations: The Solčava Panoramic Road is a quite beautiful 23 mile (37km) day-drive within easy reach of Bled – see www.solcavska-panoramska-cesta.si/en.

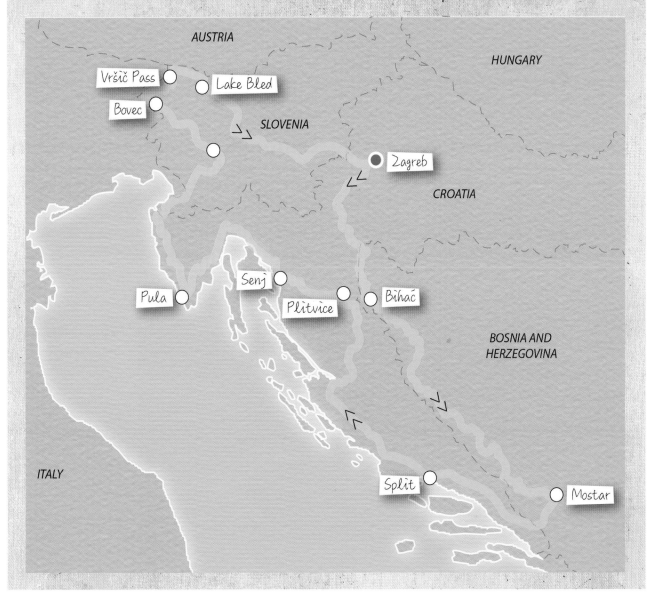

One great thing about Wales is that you can travel right across it, from the south-east to the north-west corner, almost entirely on fantastic driving roads. And even if you might, on occasion, get stuck behind a caravan or tractor then there's always something to look at out the window; from bucolic vistas and sleepy market towns to spectacular mountains and raging rivers.

I had thought about this route, Chepstow to Anglesey, as the trip for Wales, but there are a few ways through Snowdonia, you wouldn't really want to miss the coast, and can you really say you've visited the principality without going to the capital, Cardiff?

Entering Wales along the older and much more characterful of the two Severn bridges it's a short drive to where the fun starts on the fantastic B4235 between Chepstow and Usk. From Usk there are some brisk, flowing roads to the foodie town of Abergaveny and then it's on into the Brecon Beacons (Brecon). Then, after Llandovery, it's time for one of my favourite roads, the A482 to Lampeter, from where there's a really twisting and sometimes narrow drive to Devil's Bridge (A485; B4343) before a wonderful blat to the coast at Aberystwyth (A4120).

From Aber' it's on to Machynlleth and as soon as you cross the stone bridge over the Dyfi the character of the landscape begins to change, as you're now in Snowdonia; the road dramatically climbing alongside the majestic Cader Idris. Head towards Dolgellau, then Bala, where the route skirts the edge of the lake of the same name, and then on to the Llanberis Pass – you're unlikely to get this road to yourself but there's enough drama in the scenery to make up for that.

Anglesey's a great place to spend a night before heading south from Caernarfon (castle) along the A4085, where the

▲ **A wet Welsh corner on the way from Devil's Bridge to Aberystwyth on the A4120, just one of a number of great driving roads on this route.** *(Bresmedia)*

road snakes between stone walls and runs alongside the delightful Blaenau Ffestiniog steam railway for some of the way.

It's all about the coast from here; visit Portmeirion (a little slice of Italy in the heart of Wales and the setting for the cult sixties TV series *The Prisoner*), Harlech (castle); Barmouth and Aberdyfi, before retracing your wheel-tracks between Mach' and Aber', rejoining the coast road to take in Aberaeron (picture perfect pastel terraced houses); Cardigan and on to Pembrokeshire, where the route takes in the delights of St Davids (Britain's smallest city with its wonderful cathedral), Solva and Pendine Sands – where once heroes such as Malcolm Campbell set their speed records along the beach.

It's a short drive from there to the stunning Gower Peninsula and Swansea, and then just half an hour along the M4 to buzzing Cardiff.

◀ **Pendine Sands is still used for record breaking – this 1,200bhp Porsche 911 is pictured before a high-speed run.** *(Zef Eisenberg Madmax Race Team)*

PLANNING NOTES

Start and finish: Chepstow (though this is a loop so you could begin in the north or even pick up a hire car in Cardiff).
Distance: 640 miles (1,030km).
Time needed: There's enough to see and do to fill a week.
When to go: Autumn's great for avoiding the crowds.
Vehicle: A bit of power would help up the hills – and with overtaking.

Beware of: Welsh police have a reputation for being strict on speeding, so watch out for speed traps.
Detours, extensions and variations: This route incorporates or runs close to some legendary driving roads including the Evo Triangle (from Cerrigydrudion – near Bala – along the A5, and then the A543 and B4501 to complete the triangle) and Black Mountain, accessible from Llandovery (Llangadog to Brynamman).

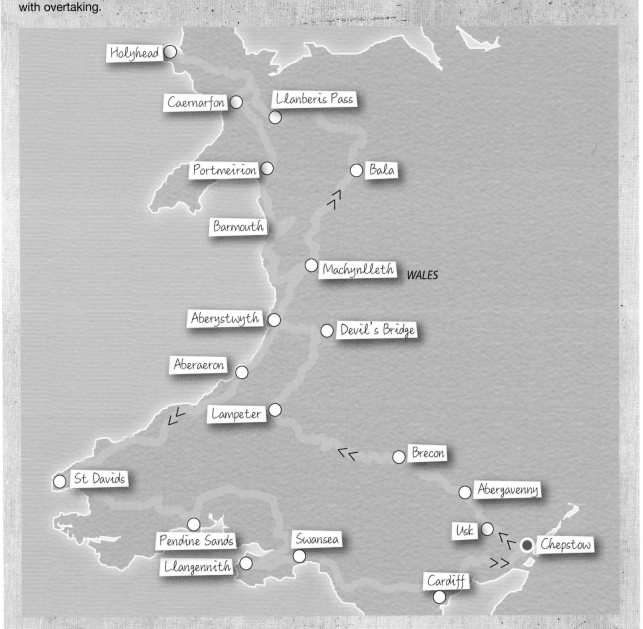

You could fly into Malaga and spend a week sitting on a beach, drinking John Smith's and eating fry-ups for breakfast. Or, you could fly into Malaga, pick up a hire car and spend a week visiting some of the most fascinating cities in Europe, exploring impressive historic buildings, drinking Fino sherry and nibbling on tasty tapas delights while watching and listening to spirited flamenco. Tough choice? Then you're probably reading the wrong book.

But if you do like the sound of the latter option then there's an easy loop around Andalusia that takes in the very best of Moorish architecture and moreish food. Starting at Malaga airport (Seville if you prefer), driven anti-clockwise the loop takes you along the coast – by way of Almuñécar with its well-known beaches and San Miguel Castle, complete with skeleton in the dungeon – and then north to Granada (and the incomparable Alhambra Palace), then on via the often bypassed but interesting, church-packed Antequera, to Córdoba (which has its fair share of Moorish sites such as the Mesquita mosque/cathedral plus a burgeoning food scene), then Seville (with one of the most impressive cathedrals you will ever visit and the beguiling Alcázar Palace).

Seville is also, arguably, the best place in Spain for a proper tapas experience; but the 'arguably' stems from the

▶ One of the best things about this trip is the food and drink, especially in a Seville tapas bar like this.
(Radiokafka / Shutterstock Shutterstock)

▲ There aren't many places that can top Ronda when it comes to dramatic locations. *(Shutterstock)*

fact that all the other Andalusian towns and cities would claim the same. I recommend pinchos morunos; kebabs which pack that punch of spice to remind you that this place was once as much Middle Eastern as European, in terms of influence at least. They go well with ice cold Cruzcampo.

But it's not just palaces, tapas and beer, and one of the highlights of this trip is Ronda. This is a mountaintop white town set above a deep gorge, the El Tajo, which separates the city's circa-15th century new town from its old town, the latter dating back to Moorish times. Puente Nuevo, a

stone bridge, is the most dramatic of the three that span the gorge and connect the two parts of the town. There's more to Ronda than its teetering clifftop location, though, with enough to do and see to warrant an overnight stay before closing off the loop in Malaga, visiting the dramatic El Chorro gorge on the way.

You needn't go straight back to the airport in Malaga, either, for while it might be known for its high-rise hotels the Malagueños are justly proud of their fresh fish restaurants while it also has its own Moorish sites, plus a great Picasso museum – the artist was born here. A perfect loop might not be quite the later Picasso's style, but it certainly describes this trip.

PLANNING NOTES

Start and finish: Malaga.
Distance: 466 miles (750km).
Time needed: Around a week to ten days; try to allow for at least a couple of nights in each of the main cities.
When to go: Andalusia is a year-round destination so why not try this for some winter sun, though it can get cold in the mountains and it does rain in the interior. In the summer it's often hot and crowded, especially in August.
Vehicle: A hire car is adequate.
Beware of: The main problem in the old cities is parking. It tends to be available in large underground lots or multistoreys, but this is also on the expensive side – even the hotels with parking will probably charge in the city centres. Maybe think about staying on the outskirts, and certainly do your homework before choosing a place to stay.
Detours, extensions and variations: From Seville, drive there-and-back to Jerez; known as the city of flamenco, sherry, horses and motorcycles, which is a splendid combination – if a little dangerous when attempted simultaneously.

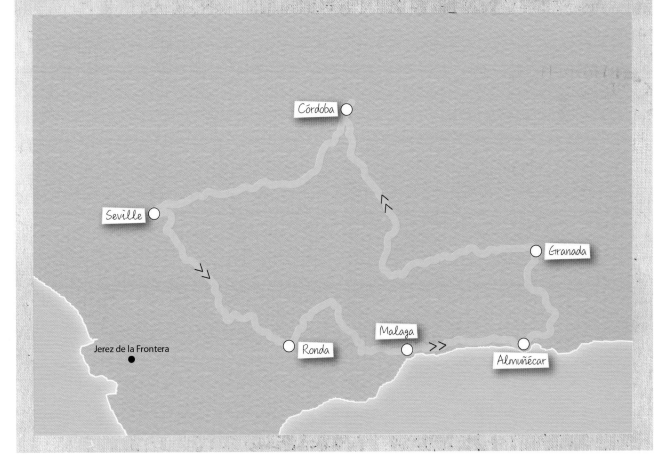

▲ **The Trollstigen National Tourist Route is just one of 18 of these dramatic scenic routes in Norway.**
(Samuel Taipale/visitnorway.com)

I n Douglas Adams's *Hitchhiker's Guide to the Galaxy* we read that Slartibartfast designed the coastline of Norway with its 'lovely crinkly edges'. He even won an award for it. Crinkly edges aren't loved by roadbuilders, of course, but then they do make for great driving roads. Which is just one of the reasons Norway's National Tourist Routes are certainly worthy of mention in the 'Roadtrippers Guide to the Galaxy'.

The National Tourist Routes are 18 of the best scenic drives in Norway, and around ten of these are either part of or within easy reach of this trip, which runs from Stavanger (visit the iconic Pulpit Rock which is not far from the city) to lively Trondheim.

For full details of the National Tourist Routes see the websites in the Planning notes opposite, but of those this trip features the Hardanger route, between Låtefossen (with its spectacular waterfall) and Granvin, a fjord-hugging treat, while the Sognefjellet National Tourist Route, from Gaupne

◄ **It's not all staggering natural beauty in Norway, there's some seriously impressive manmade stuff too – this is a portion of the Atlantic Road.** *(Shutterstock)*

to Lom, is northern Europe's highest road that's over a mountain pass; 1,430m (4,691ft) with suitably breathtaking scenery. And let's not forget the Trollstigen National Tourist Route, between Valldalen and Åndalsnes – a hairpin-riven zigzag that runs close to the 1,900m (6,230ft) Troll Wall (Trollvegen in Norwegian), which is the tallest vertical rock face in Europe.

If you get bored with the natural wonders Norway has to offer – you won't – then there's a manmade marvel to ogle, and better still, drive. The Atlantic Road runs from Vevang to Kårvåg, and although it stretches for just five and a bit miles it's one of the most famous drives on the planet. This series of serpentine bridges and causeways links a string of tiny islands, with the Storseisundet Bridge the most spectacular

of the crossings – it's especially fun, or challenging, to drive when there's a storm crashing in off the Atlantic.

Many of the National Tourist Routes are closed in the winter, but the spine of this route still offers much, including the Laerdal Tunnel between Aurlandsvangen and Lærdalsøyri, which is the world's longest road tunnel and features an ever-changing lighting effect to simulate a sunny day in the heart of the mountain. It also has four vast rock chambers along its 15.5 mile (26km) length for subterranean pit stops. Mind you, you might prefer the Snow Road, the Aurlandsfjellet National Tourist Route, which runs over the top, but this is usually only open in the summer months. Either way it puts a whole new slant on taking the high road or the low road.

PLANNING NOTES

Start and finish: Stavanger to Trondheim.
Distance: 620 miles (1,000km).
Time needed: A week to ten days.
When to go: If you want to drive as many of the National Routes as possible then summer is best. It goes without saying that winter is very cold, while many of the National Routes will be closed.
Vehicle: Hire cars are available, though they are very expensive in Norway, so driving your own car in from another part of Europe could be worthwhile.
Beware of: Norway is not a cheap country to visit – the price of beer is criminal!
Detours, extensions and variations: To avoid a steep drop-off fee and also see a lot more of the country, why not add around 746 miles (1,200km) and drive along the coast from Oslo to Stavanger, then take the direct route from Trondheim to Oslo, crossing the spectacular high country of central Norway?
Further information: www.nasjonaleturistveger.no/en/routes and www.fjordnorway.com.

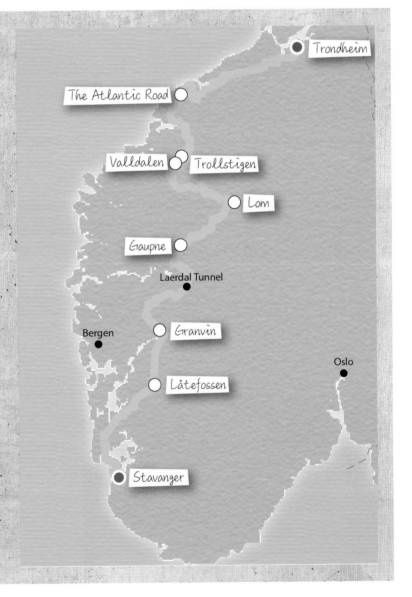

▲ **Our little Polo parked in front of a Communist-era sculpture in Bulgaria.** *(Bresmedia)*

With driving, like cooking, sometimes slow is best. Especially if you really want to soak up the flavour of a country, or even a continent. In 2004 we spent £300 on an ancient Volkswagen Polo (see The basics) and set off to explore Europe for three months. We actually saw a lot of Turkey, too (see Asia) but for the purposes of this chapter we will concentrate on Istanbul and back, as that really is the far edge of the continent if you're travelling from northern Europe.

As we set out in March and we were planning on camping – the price of the car alone should have warned you this was a budget trip – the first priority was to get to the sun as quickly as possible. The route went through France and Switzerland – at this time of the year the passes are still closed but this does give you the opportunity to experience the amazing Gotthard Tunnel, which burrows for 10.5 miles (16.9km) under the Alps.

Once we had flown south this was not about rushing, we had plenty of time, which meant if we found a campsite we liked and the weather was good, we stayed put for a little while – Capitolo in Puglia, Italy and idyllic Kato Gatzea on the Pelion Peninsula, Greece, were memorable longish stops.

We got to Greece on the overnight ferry from Italy, but at other times of the year maybe a trip through the Balkans would be better. After Greece and the European part of Turkey it was into Eastern Europe, which was still changing back then, and it was the reminders of the Communist past that stick in the memory most. Our route took us up through Bulgaria and into Romania, then into Hungary, Slovakia, the Czech Republic, and from there into Germany and on to the Netherlands, Belgium, France and back to the UK.

This trip won't be quite the same these days, yet in many ways now is the perfect time to drive this route, or something similar. There really is no better way to truly get to know Europe and, more to the point, there is no better way to get to know the people of Europe.

◄ **If you're road tripping on a budget then nothing beats camping – this is our set-up in Puglia, Italy.** *(Bresmedia)*

PLANNING NOTES

Start and finish: London.
Distance: 5,000 miles (8,000km): note that only cities are shown on the map as it's impossible to mark all the stops.
Time needed: As long as you've got; this is not one for rushing.
When to go: Summer is probably best if you're camping.
Vehicle: If you're using an old car or camper, you might want to check on emissions restrictions for some cities.

Beware of: You're taking it easy, so no need to worry about much at all. Mind you, you don't really want to camp every night, so treat yourself to a hotel every now and then.

Detours, extensions and variations: Wherever the road takes you, but a loop through Poland, Lithuania, Latvia, Estonia, Finland, Sweden, Denmark and then back to Germany would be a great addition to this.

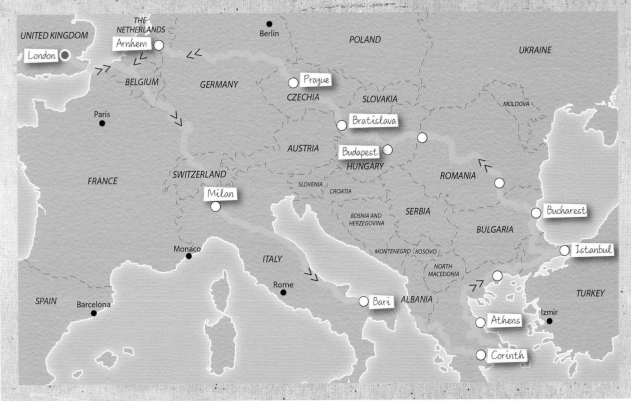

BY THE WAY ...

Roadside Mig

When we were driving through Eastern Europe a few years back some of the most interesting things we stumbled upon were the remnants from the Communist and Cold War past, whether it was old Stalinist memorials or brutally stark architecture, or on one occasion by the roadside in the Solt area in Hungary this seemingly abandoned and very battered MiG-15 jet fighter. Wonder if it's still there?

Chapter 3

NORTH AMERICA

Hear the words 'road trip' and the image that will likely leap into your mind is of a lonely and straight desert road diminishing to a tiny point on the horizon in the United States. The road trip is part of American folklore, the afterglow of the burning spirit that took people west, and the best way to see this vast land by far. But it's not all about arrow-straight roads as the USA and Canada also have some of the world's best mountain and coastal drives. The car was made for America, it's been said, and America was certainly made for the car.

▶ **Mountain road in Colorado.** *(Shutterstock)*

Route 66 represents the very essence of the American road trip, cutting through eight US states in 2,500 miles packed with quirkiness, calories and – of course – kicks.

Route 66 is the quintessential road trip. It's the sort of thing people say they want to do even if they don't really know what it is. What it actually is is a monument; a testament to that old American dream of loading up the car and heading over the horizon to find fame and fortune.

Also known as the Mother Road, Main Street of America and the Will Rogers Highway, Route 66 came into being in 1926, with road signs along its length springing up the following year. This most famous of American roads

▼ **The old Route 66 route marker is as an American icon.**
(Bresmedia)

▼ **Easy rider: a straight road to the horizon and a motorcycle, it doesn't get more Route 66 than this.** *(Bresmedia)*

stretched for 2,448 miles (3,940km) starting in Chicago and finishing in Santa Monica, Los Angeles and visiting Illinois, Missouri, Kansas, Oklahoma, Texas, New Mexico and Arizona along the way to California.

The Mother Road is almost 100 now, so more a great-great-grandmother, and during her time she's seen the migrations of the 1930s' depression and then the growth and subsequent demise of communities along her length as younger, sexier, faster interstates took her place. The road also became something of an icon through song and film, which is part of the reason many seek their kicks on Route 66 long after this was the best way to go way out west.

It actually ceased to be an official highway in 1985, though large parts of it are now known and shown on maps as Historic Route 66. And, as we said above, that's just what this is; a drive through history.

Our trip was also some time ago now, but the great thing about nostalgia is that while it's not what it used to be, things tend to stay the same. In fact, maybe it gets a little better, as the quirky diners and motels are spruced up a little to attract and cater for the new breed of Route 66 traveller.

Many do Route 66 on a motorcycle or in a convertible, but we could afford neither option, mainly because the drop-off fee we had to pay was astronomical – it's not always so bad if you do this as a package, but we were going on to New York – and so we ticked the box for an economy

BY THE WAY ...

Cadillac ranch

This famous art installation, on Route 66 just outside Amarillo (yes, this is the way), was set up in 1974. It's free of charge and it's always open; just park up and walk right in. The partly interred Cadillacs date from a 1948 model to a 1963 example and they're usually covered in graffiti. If Cadillacs aren't your thing then further along Route 66 and still within the Texas Panhandle at Conway is the Bug Ranch, a similar theme, only this time with VW Beetles.

model. But, maybe because of lack of demand the other side of the country for transcontinental shopping-cars, we were upgraded to a biggish, white, softly-sprung Chevrolet Monte Carlo. It was like driving a cloud as we floated out of Santa Monica.

I will admit that we lost Route 66 on a few occasions on that first day, but never for too long, and while there was always something interesting to ogle at, it was great to quite suddenly feel we had broken free of the Los Angeles conurbation to hit Route 66 proper, especially on the stretch from Victorville to Barstow, passing through cowboy film-like scenery – you will have gathered by now we were doing this in the 'wrong' direction, but it works both ways and the signs show the way east as well as west.

In the spirit of this sort of journey we decided to find our accommodation as we went. This was usually in motels, as much an icon of the American road trip as the Route 66 sign itself. Our first stop was in Barstow, still in California, in a place with an atmospheric dead car park and neon signage; pure 66. Finding accommodation as you go seems the essence of freedom, but freedom also means allowing yourself to stray, to cut the apron strings of the Mother Road from time to time. And you can't really ignore Las Vegas – it won't let you!

A day or two later and back on 66 it was effortless desert driving, the motorised meditation that makes these trips so wonderful. Also wonderful was the little Western town of Seligman, which can claim to be the birthplace of Historic Route 66 back in the 1980s. When the nearby interstate opened in 1978 Seligman all but withered on

▼ Route 66 has more than its fair share of evocative places to stop for lunch. *(Bresmedia)*

▼ Abandoned gas stations and ghost towns are part of the poignant charm of Route 66. *(Bresmedia)*

the vine, but now it thrives as a sort of living museum; largely thanks to the efforts of local barber and Route 66 legend Angel Delgadillo. Our next overnight was at Williams, another place stuffed with interesting Route 66 memorabilia, which is also just a short drive to a must-do detour, the Grand Canyon.

The Grand Canyon was certainly grand enough, but all the same it was good to get back on 66. A few days in and the bug for the road had bitten and seeing that familiar sign again was a real tonic. The appeal? For me, the poignancy of derelict gas stations and 'ghost towns' such as Newkirk, New Mexico and Glenrio, Texas, which seem like islands cut off from the flow of time as much as the flow of traffic. And then there are the early alignments of 66 that were bypassed so long ago that they remain dirt roads; such as the stretch that includes the charismatic bridge at Querino Canyon.

Actually, following these different alignments and also trying to find certain sections of Route 66 is part of the challenge of this trip. They say there's about 85% of the route that's still easily driveable, but it's no use using a satnav, that will just keep taking you back onto the Mother Road's nemesis, the interstate. Luckily, there are books and apps that help, but you will also need to do a bit of detective work on occasion. It's why this is still an adventure.

Sometimes, rather forlornly, the old road runs parallel to the interstates that led to its demise, and on occasion it's worth skipping over on to the freeway, just to make up time when you need to, though it's always quite a wrench to leave the older, weather-crazed, asphalt.

It is certainly worth straying just a little way from 66 in Arizona, though, to see the Painted Desert and the Petrified Forest; the latter pieces of trees now turned to rock. I don't think I've ever seen a sky as that which ballooned over the Painted Desert. There was one single cloud that day, and its shadow looked like a flat dark island on a sea of colour: reds, browns, ochres, lavender, purple and everything in between. It was like stepping into a vast Van Gogh.

There was plenty more of interest in Arizona, and New Mexico was the same. We spent a memorable evening shooting pool in a cliché one-storey bar with a rank of pickup trucks parked outside in Grants, and also had a fine lunch of Navajo burger in Gallup – the bread it came on, not in, was somewhere between a Yorkshire pudding and a naan and is called Indian fry bread. I'm not sure it's good for the arteries, but then an American road trip seldom is.

On that score it's worth noting that portions are big in the US. Very big. And the food is often pretty good, too. Culinary highlights included the Mexican food in New Mexico, naturally, especially at Joseph's in Santa Rosa. It was so good we stayed over and had breakfast there: eggs, rye toast, sausage and hash browns with a never-ending cup of coffee, which set us up for the drive in to the Texas Panhandle.

God is omnipresent, some still say, but nowhere is that more so than in the Texan plains. 'The biggest Cross in the Western Hemisphere' was just one reminder, as was the local radio ad' 'Cleaning carpets for the glory of God since 1987', or something like that. Actually, one of the great joys of an American road trip is the radio, allowing it to do its thing, latching on to whatever station it finds as you go. At one point there was live coverage of a chilli cook off. It seemed like a big deal, the amount of airtime it was given,

▼ An early alignment of R66 in Arizona took us on to a dirt road and over the Querino Canyon Bridge. *(Bresmedia)*

▼ The U Drop Inn in Shamrock, Texas. *(Bresmedia)*

▲ **Moving house; literally. We were stuck behind this for quite a while as we crossed the Texas Panhandle.** *(Bresmedia)*

▲ **Here it is! You'll need to drive Route 66 to find out what.** *(Bresmedia)*

then we drove right past it, a small gathering in a tiny field, and a minute later the radio switched to a channel covering a baseball match. It's a big country, the US, but on many levels so small.

Yet always surprising. Still in Texas, we were held up for quite a while by someone moving house. Literally. A whole house, and a fair-sized one at that, three bedrooms at the very least, trundling down the road in front of us at about 5mph – on a trailer of some kind I should add – overspilling both lanes. Of course, once the novelty wore off we were stuck behind the thing for ages, while the traffic on the interstate that ran parallel to this stretch of 66 just 50m (165ft) or so away zapped by at warp speed.

We were about ready for a beer by the time we arrived at McLean, a small town known for its barbed wire, or 'Devil's Rope', museum. The woman at the motel was very friendly, so, thirsty for local knowledge on McLean's saloons, we asked where the best was to be found. The atmosphere suddenly turned as frosty as the cold suds we'd hoped to be sipping as we were told that McLean, Texas (I don't know why but you really need to add the 'Texas') was dry. We found a place that did a fabulous steak – as big as a laptop but it would have been better with a nice drop of Malbec – and spent a Friday night on the wagon. When we returned to the motel the landlady had made a point of opening the Bible that sat on the bedside table to a page that spoke about the evils of alcohol and debauchery.

We didn't get to see the Devil's Rope museum – to be honest I've read too much on the First World War to think it's a thing worth celebrating, they should turn it into a bar

– but it is often listed as one of those Route 66 oddities that are a hugely enjoyable feature of driving this trip. When the road was in its pomp motels, diners and gas stations vied for travellers' dollars with ever more ingenious ways to entice eyes away from the long road ahead (see By the way overleaf), while there are also other attractions that have sprouted up as a result of Route 66's rebirth as a 'destination' in its own right, such as the world's biggest rocking chair in Missouri (though its claim is controversial and it might well be the second biggest now).

The Missouri town of Cuba's Route 66 claim to fame is its pristine water tower, and it's also a nice place to stay. Our motel here was over the freeway, so we needed to cross a bridge to find a place to eat. As we walked along the side of the road, there was no sidewalk, we realised that we were getting very funny looks from passing motorists. I had to quickly check that I hadn't left the motel naked (again!), but it wasn't that. I think, in the end, the weird thing we were doing was walking. We had seen the many drive-in restaurants, drive-in banks and drive-in barbers (okay, I made the last one up, but why not?) but it was in Cuba where the US's centaur-like attachment to the car really hit home.

On through Missouri, crossing the Mississippi and passing the impressive Gateway Arch at St Louis, and in many places the old stretches of 66 began to take on another character, a wonderfully neglected feel, with grass growing through the concrete slabs, but there were also plenty of lovingly restored diners and gas stations as we headed north now, with charming towns like Pontiac to explore before the end of the Mother Road.

BY THE WAY ...

Manic street features

One of the hallmarks of Route 66 is its quirky roadside attractions. They date from a time when competition for the traveller's dollar was intense, and each town, hotel and diner along the way strived to stand out. They are all worth a stop – if only to smile and shake your head. Here are some favourites:

1. Gemini Giant, Wilmington Illinois *(Bresmedia)*.
2. Paul Bunyon Hot Dog, Atlanta Illinois *(Bresmedia)*.
3. Twin Arrows, Arizona *(Shutterstock)*.
4. Wigwam Motel, Holbrook, Arizona *(Alberto Loyo / Shutterstock)*.

▶ **Some 3,200 miles (5,150km) done and about as many splattered bugs to prove it. Our Chevy in New York at the end of the trip.** *(Bresmedia)*

In retrospect I regret not stopping at Chicago, instead we drove to the sign that marked the finishing line for Route 66, then turned right at Lake Michigan, towards New York. That was it for 66, then. But we still had another 800 miles (1,287km) to go before we reached the Big Apple. It was pretty exciting going over George Washington Bridge and then on to Manhattan; just like much of this road trip it was like driving into a movie. A movie that needs a rerun soon.

PLANNING NOTES

Start and finish: Chicago to Santa Monica (or the other way around as we did it; we also carried on east to finish in New York).

Distance: The current length is around 2,400 miles (3,860km) – though this can vary depending on how strict you are in following the original route and which alignments you follow.

Time needed: Three weeks is about right for Route 66 but a fortnight is possible.

When to go: In the height of summer, July and August, both temperatures and prices can be high – the former dramatically so in the desert areas. April to June and the end of August through to the end of October work well.

Vehicle: Anything goes, really, and while a Harley (and there are companies which hire out motorcycles especially for this trip) or a drop-top Mustang fit the picture well, something more run of the mill might fit the wallet better.

Beware of: Navigation is likely to be your biggest issue. Satnavs will try to take you on to the interstate at every intersection so you will want to make use of one of the many books (*Route 66: EZ66 Guide for Travelers* by Jerry McClanahan is good) and apps that are available.

Detours, extensions and variations: The obvious detours are Las Vegas and the Grand Canyon but Santa Fe – actually on a variation of Route 66 – is also well worth a visit.

Further information: www.historic66.com

A visit to Alcatraz, the infamous old prison on an island in San Francisco Bay, is certainly recommended, not least because it reminds you that you are indeed free. And how better to express that freedom than embarking on one of the US's best-known road trips?

The road that runs along the coast of California is called Coastal Highway 1; the convention is that it's referred to as the Pacific Coast Highway south of San Francisco, Highway 1 to the north, though this seems to be interchangeable depending on who you speak to so I will stick with Highway 1 here. In its entirety this route stretches from Seattle in the north to San Diego in the south, which is a great trip, but it's more common for road trippers to travel the 450 mile (725km) stretch between San Francisco and Los Angeles.

This is actually quite well known as a driver's road, but to be honest there's often a fair bit of slow-moving traffic, so

▲ Big Sur's Bixby Bridge is an icon of the coast road between San Francisco and LA. *(Shutterstock)*

on that score it can be frustrating, but on the other hand the reason the traffic is going so slowly is because of the views, particularly on the section between Monterey and Morro Bay.

Highlights along the route include San Francisco itself; Santa Cruz (seaside fun with a boardwalk, classic roller coaster and surfing); nautical Monterey (take a detour to follow 17 Mile Drive at Pebble Beach) and Carmel (10 miles, or 16km, south of which is the Point Lobos State Natural Reserve with its sea lions); then it's Big Sur, with its glorious coastline, the much-photographed Bixby Bridge, plus majestic redwood forests and top notch hiking – staying in a wood cabin here was the cherry on the cake.

The road will then take you from cabin to palace in 65 gently twisting miles (105km). Hearst Castle, once the home of publishing magnate William Randolph Hearst, is a temple to excess with 165 rooms, 127 acres of garden and even a few zebra strolling around the grounds. Even if you're not a fan of big old houses, this is pretty much a must-see, but at busy times you might need to book ahead for a tour.

On our trip we spent a night in San Luis Obispo at The Madonna Inn – wonderfully kitsch, with 110 themed rooms – before heading to chic Santa Barbara, sometimes called 'The American Riviera'. After that there's plenty to see and do in LA; an exciting place in which to end this classic road trip.

◄ The Neptune Pool is as understated as the rest of Hearst Castle. *(Joseph Sohm / Shutterstock)*

PLANNING NOTES

Start and finish: San Francisco to Los Angeles.

Distance: 450 miles (724km).

Time needed: There's much to see and this could fill a week to ten days easily, though the great thing is the route itself is short enough that you could also do it much quicker, if you felt the need, and still see the highlights. Leave time for exploring the two amazing cities at the start and finish, though.

When to go: California's a year-round destination with dry summers and some rain in the winter, but the famous sea fog which can be a feature from July to September can spoil the views. September to October is not so busy, while the weather's still pretty good.

Vehicle: Pretty much any car will do, while the part of the route between Monterey and Morro Bay is reckoned to be one of the best motorcycle rides in the USA.

Beware of: In 2017 a landslide in the Big Sur area caused the road to close for 14 months and when it rains heavily smaller scale landslides are not uncommon. Luckily there's usually an interesting inland detour to follow (to check, go to dot.ca.gov/cgi-bin/roads.cgi).

Detours, extensions and variations: There are so many ways to make more of this; travelling north from San Francisco to Seattle; further south to San Diego, or looping around from LA back to San Francisco via Las Vegas, Death Valley and Yosemite, are just some of the great options.

San Francisco

Santa Cruz

Monterey

Big Sur

Hearst Castle

San Luis Obispo

Santa Barbara

Los Angeles

One thing we had expected on our Canadian road trip was wilderness and it was remarkable how soon after we had left Vancouver it was just us, the road, trees and mountains. One thing we hadn't really expected was wine, yet our first stop was in Kelowna, a fun place on the eastern shore of Okanagan Lake, which is surrounded by vineyards.

From then on it was pretty much as anticipated, though, only more so, particularly after we arrived at Wells Gray Provincial Park. Some of the 39 named waterfalls here are truly stunning (Helmcken Falls, Dawson Falls and Spahats Falls are especially accessible on a good gravel road but don't lack for awe because of this).

And then there's the bears. At first we just saw their droppings – in the woods, of course – as we hiked, which was exciting, but later we also saw a couple of them from the car. To be honest I got a bit obsessed with trying to spot them after that, even the clouds started to look like skydiving bears. But maybe that was the Canadian wine?

From Clearwater it was on to Jasper in Alberta on an uncrowded Southern Yellowhead Highway (Highway 5) with the wild North Thompson River and achingly impressive scenery for company for much of the way. Jasper was spectacular, with some more bear sightings, including cubs, plus a moose, some elk and a fleeting glimpse of a coyote, and great hiking around glacier-fed aquamarine lakes and through sun-dappled forests.

To be fair, there's not much in the way of boring scenery on this trip, but even Canada outdid itself on the next stage of

▲ Helmcken is just one of a number of outrageously spectacular waterfalls in Wells Gray Provincial Park. *(Bresmedia)*

▼ Canadian road trips have an obvious appeal. *(Bresmedia)*

the journey; the Icefields Parkway. This is a 146 mile (235km) route between Jasper and Lake Louise which, with its turquoise lakes, myriad waterfalls and the glaciers it's named for, is perhaps one of the most amazing drives in the world.

One of the many highlights is going out on to the Athabasca Glacier, which means taking a bus ride with a difference in one of the special giant-wheeled Ice Explorers, which take you to a place where you can explore the glacier on foot with the reassuring knowledge that it's 360m (1,180ft) thick.

Lake Louise offers yet more stunning views, and then it's an easy drive to Banff, a place with an adventurous feel to it and a great base for hiking. It's then a short journey to cowboy town Calgary to celebrate the trip with excellent fillet steak – and maybe a glass of that Canadian wine to wash it down with.

PLANNING NOTES

Start and finish: Vancouver to Calgary.
Distance: 870 miles (1,400km).
Time needed: For the trip outlined here a little over a week, plus a couple of days in Vancouver and one in Calgary (12 in total) was fine.
When to go: It's always best to have the road as much to yourself as possible so the shoulder seasons make sense. September is said to be good, but we went in late May, which was perfect. Summer's best, but accommodation prices can rocket in line with demand, and it is, of course, snowy in winter.

Vehicle: A regular hire car, available in Vancouver with drop-off in Calgary, but an RV would work very well – these are popular choices in this part of Canada, so make sure you book early.
Beware of: Canada's one of the safest countries in the world – the biggest danger will be crashing into the back of another car while distracted by some amazing scenery. Oh, but best be careful with those bears, too.
Detours, extensions and variations: You could drive to Whistler along the stunning Sea to Sky Highway (99), and then head to Wells Gray Provincial Park from there before continuing with the route as described.

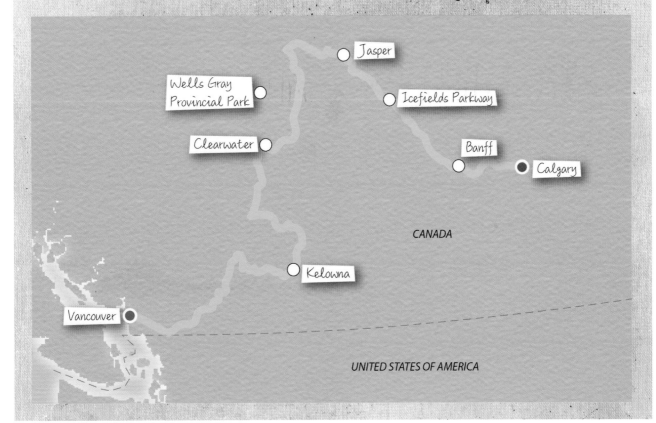

Jasper

Wells Gray Provincial Park

Icefields Parkway

Clearwater

Banff

Calgary

CANADA

Kelowna

Vancouver

UNITED STATES OF AMERICA

While this drive around the Gaspé Peninsula is a classic coastal loop, lassoing out into the Gulf of St Lawrence, part of the attraction is also the sparsely populated interior, where there are untamed rivers, towering peaks and all the things that make Canada such a great place for an adventure.

That's not to say this 684 mile (1,100km) trip, which follows Route 132 and is easily accessible from Quebec City and Montreal (a one-and-a-half and four-hour drive from the start respectively) is not a wonderful journey in its own right, though, as it certainly is, with rugged scenery, thick green forests skirting the sea, and dramatic rock-scapes.

Starting at La Pocatière on the south side of the St Lawrence River the route takes you, via some beautiful villages in the Kamouraska area, to Rivière-du-Loup (for whale watching cruises), Rimouski, Amqui and New Richmond; then it's on to the picturesque village of Percé and the stunning Percé Rock, a huge limestone formation that rises out of the sea like some rocky sea monster and which features one of the world's largest natural arches – hence the name, as Percé is 'pierce' in French. The town

▼ **Route 132 around the Gaspé Peninsula is one of Canada's best coastal drives.** *(Tourisme Québec / Sébastien Cloutier)*

▶ **Moose are common in Gaspésie, so watch out for them on the road.** *(Tourisme Québec / Michel Julien)*

of Gaspé is next, perhaps as a base for exploration into the stunning Forillon National Park, then Sainte-Anne-des-Monts (gateway to the spectacular Parc national de la Gaspésie) and on to Matane, where a detour off the loop to the Réserve faunique de Matane will give you the chance to see moose and black bear, always a thrill. From Matane the loop ends at Rimouski, where you can pick up the quicker Highway 20 to get back to Quebec City or Montreal.

PLANNING NOTES

Start and finish: La Pocatière to Rimouski.
Distance: 684 miles (1,100km).
Time needed: With so much to do and see, ten days would be good, but a week or less is possible.
When to go: If it's kayaking and whale watching you're interested in then the summer is the best time, but note that the peninsula gets very busy in the last two weeks of July, when it's a holiday in Quebec.
Vehicle: A regular hire car, available in Montreal or Quebec City, will do the job.

Beware of: The peninsula's home to moose and in a collision with one you might come off second best – they're heavy and have a high centre of gravity. The high-risk times are said to be dawn and dusk in June, July, October and November, but a moose collision can happen at any time so take heed of the warning signs.
Detours, extensions and variations: If you're coming east from Montreal then historic Quebec City is well worth a visit on the way.

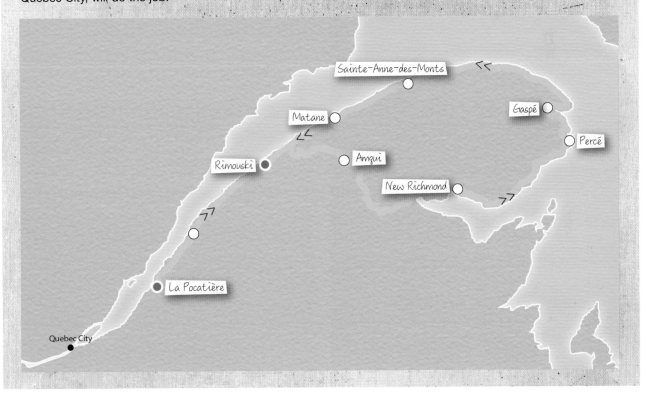

Some facts to chew on. Canada is the second-largest country in the world. The Trans-Canada Highway (TCH) traverses this vast land mass to connect the Pacific Coast with the Atlantic coast, crossing six time zones along the way. The close to 5,000 mile (8,046km) route is just 3% urban, which leaves 97% of it countryside and wilderness, and when it's Canadian countryside and wilderness then you know you're in for a treat.

And if you like to feel a certain sense of achievement after a road trip, then you might also be interested to hear that this is arguably the longest single-country highway journey in the world – the Ring Road, which traces the edge of Australia (see Oceania), might be longer, but it really depends on how you define 'continuous'. Either way, the TCH is still an epic drive.

The route runs from Victoria, British Columbia, to St John's, Newfoundland, though it can of course be driven in either direction. Along its length there are distinctive white-

▶ **Thoughtful touch: a wildlife crossing over a busy section of the Trans-Canada Highway in Banff National Park.** *(Shutterstock)*

on-green maple leaf markers that will remind you you're on the Trans-Canada Highway.

While there's undoubtedly a lot of wilderness on this route, there is still also plenty to see – in fact someone counted the points of interest as 3,500, which seems quite good value, while there are also many detours that would be hard to resist. As well as the staggeringly spectacular national parks along the TCH – such as Gros Morne, Banff and Fundy – there's the cosmopolitan capital city of Ottawa, with its excellent museums; canoeing adventures in Whiteshell Provincial Park; the Badlands scenery of the Dinosaur Provincial Park; the seemingly limitless prairies – the essence of the North American road trip – and lots more. Canada is immense and you will never get to experience it all in one bite, but with this road trip you will certainly get a very good taste of it.

▼ **The Trans-Canada Highway does exactly what it says on the sign.** *(Shutterstock)*

PLANNING NOTES

Start and finish: Victoria, British Columbia to St John's, Newfoundland (or vice versa).
Distance: 5,000 miles (8,046km).
Time needed: This is not a route to rush, there's much to see and do, and so a couple of months is probably needed to do it any justice.

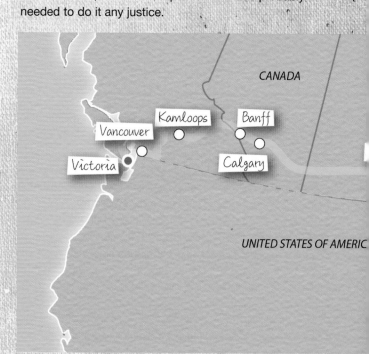

When to go: The weather in parts of Canada can be extreme so this is best done in spring, summer or early autumn.

Vehicle: It's paved all the way but you might want a 4x4 if you're planning on going off the beaten TCH.

Beware of: The weather can be unpredictable so pack accordingly and don't expect mobile phone or internet coverage everywhere. Be aware that there will be long stretches without fuel stations, so always fill up when you can.

Detours, extensions and variations: The Yellowhead Highway, a northern route through Edmonton with Prince Rupert as its western start or finish, is perhaps the most well-known of the alternative TCH routes and is also the best option if you want to avoid the prairies.

Further information: www.transcanadahighway.com

The Loneliest Road in America, unsurprisingly, is pretty much in the middle of nowhere. But then that's its appeal, while getting there and continuing on can make for an excellent road trip in its own right – but more on that later.

This stretch of the US Route 50 in Nevada gained its forlorn moniker in 1986 in a less than complimentary feature by *Life* magazine, which savvy Nevada tourism bods then spun into an advertising slogan. But despite the marketing push this still remains a lonely road.

Starting in the former stagecoach and Pony Express station of Ely in the east and ending at Fallon in the west, this 258 mile (415km) road passes through Eureka (with a population of 610, yet still boasting an opera house!); Austin (population of 192 and a self-proclaimed 'living ghost town') and Middlegate, with just a handful of people and a shoe tree, which naturally enough is a tree on which people put shoes – the original was cut down by vandals in 2010 but there is a replacement now.

▼ **Classic car show in the 'living ghost town' of Austin on the Loneliest Road.** *(TravelNevada)*

▶ **This saloon in Middlegate might just be the loneliest bar in America.** *(TravelNevada)*

At the end of the Loneliest Road – though some insist it carries on to Fernley – is Fallon, the site of Naval Air Station Fallon, the home of the Top Gun training programme since 1996.

Will the Loneliest Road 'take your breath away'? If you like desert landscapes hemmed in by distant mountains, sometimes snow-capped, then it probably will, though it's not all arrow-straight to the ruffled horizon and there are a number of small passes to negotiate, too.

There are also a few options when it comes to developing this into a much longer and perhaps more satisfying road trip. For instance, you will need to drive to Ely (240 miles, or 385km, from Salt Lake City) for a start, and then from Fallon you could stay with the lonely road theme and loop around Highways 95, 6 and 375 to Rachel, and then head to Las Vegas via Area 51 (keeping your eye on the sky). Another attractive option would be to drive to Yosemite via Carson City, then south to Death Valley NP, and then on to Vegas.

PLANNING NOTES

Start and finish: Ely to Fallon.

Distance: 258 miles (415km).

Time needed: You could easily drive this in a day, even with stops for the sights, but stretch the route west, east and south and you could have an excellent road trip of a week or more.

When to go: While parts of the road are as high as 1,400m (4,500ft) and it gets cold in winter it actually forms part of the American Defense Highway and so has to remain open and clear of snow throughout the year.

Vehicle: A hire car is fine.

Beware of: It's easy for the speed to creep up on long, straight roads, and it's not so lonely that there are no police around. Do what Americans do, engage cruise control.

Detours, extensions and variations: If you're starting your journey in Salt Lake City then you could stop at Wendover where it's possible to drive on the Bonneville Salt Flats, if there are no speed trials or record attempts in progress.

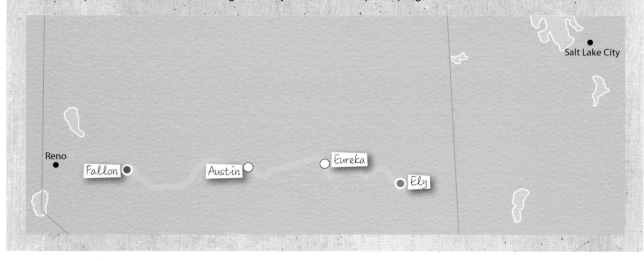

New England is justly famous for its spectacular autumns, nature's silent firework display; flaming vermilion, scarlet, purple, orange and bronze.

It's a free show, too. Well, up to a point, you still need to pay for your trip and parts of New England can be a more expensive destination in the autumn. Indeed, the demand is such that hotel and guest house owners will sometimes insist on a minimum two-night stay, something that can prove restrictive when the drive is as important as the 'leaf peeping' – yes, that's what looking at trees in the fall is called. With that in mind, a fly-drive pre-booked package is not a bad option for this one, and there are plenty available.

It's not all about colourful foliage, though, and a good two-week, five-state road trip could cover so much more. This would start at Boston, Massachusetts (American history and excellent clam chowder) and then head to Providence, Rhode Island (wineries on the way and history and fine dining in the town); then west to charming Stockbridge and Lenox via Old Sturbridge Village, said to be the largest outdoor museum in the north east of the US. From there it's north out of Connecticut and into Vermont and the historic villages of Bennington and Manchester – the top of Mount Equinox offers excellent views – then Burlington, on Lake Champlain, before crossing over into New Hampshire and Franconia

▲ **Covered bridges are a hallmark of New England – this one is in Flume Gorge State Park, Franconia, New Hampshire.** *(Shutterstock)*

Notch State Park and the spectacular Flume Gorge. From there you would take the amazing Kancamagus Highway from Lincoln to North Conway (Highway 112); a good base for hiking and other activities in the rugged White Mountains.

From North Conway it's back to the coast in Maine, heading to historic Portland and a stay at the Old Port, then continuing along US Route 1 with a string of picturesque coastal towns to explore – don't miss the lobster at Boothbay Harbor – before arriving at elegant Portsmouth, from where it's an easy and interesting drive back to Boston. Even without the autumn colours that would be quite a trip.

▼ **The drive described here is as much about the coast as the autumn colours – this is Portland Head lighthouse.** *(Jenny Campbell/Maine Office of Tourism)*

PLANNING NOTES

Start and finish: Boston.

Distance: 700 miles (1,120km).

Time needed: Two weeks would be good, just because there are so many diversions, but make sure to allow for a couple of days in Boston.

When to go: If you're not bothered about the autumn colour then late May to early July is an ideal time for this trip, but high summer can be crowded, expensive and humid. Winters can be severe in New England.

Vehicle: Boston is well-served with hire car companies.

Beware of: If you're set on seeing the spectacular foliage then think about booking ahead, and even if you're not some guest houses might stipulate a two-night minimum stay on the weekends.

Detours, extensions and variations: The fabulous mansions at Newport, Rhode Island will be hard to resist, while Cape Cod has something for everyone.

(Shutterstock)

Some say to understand the Mississippi is to understand the USA itself, and there are few better ways of understanding Old Man River than driving the length of it. The Great River Road (often abbreviated to GRR) follows the course of this most famous of American rivers for 1,500 miles (2,400km), from Minnesota to the Gulf of Mexico across ten states. That's pretty much the USA north to south, driving through the throbbing heart of America.

The GRR is actually a network of roads that are spliced together to form a contiguous route and its green route signs feature a boat's wheel and a paddle steamer, an icon of the great river – these are not easy to find in every state but there's a helpful app for navigation (see Planning notes).

Because interstates tend to go in straight lines the GRR has survived the march of progress as they have passed it by. This means that as you mirror the meanderings of the Mississippi you will discover seemingly forgotten towns, cut off like islands in the river itself. There's also good food and foot-tapping music, verdant forests, mysterious swamps, towering limestone cliffs, the Mid west prairies, cotton fields, and quite a few parks. The GRR also has its fair share of Route 66 style kitsch – like the world's largest six-pack of beer in La Crosse, or the biggest boot, in Red Wing. Yet

▲ **The Great River Road intersects with Route 66 at St Louis, where the famous arch is just one of the attractions.** *(Shutterstock)*

▼ **The paddle steamer is an icon of the river – this one is pictured in New Orleans, at the end of the GRR.** *(Shutterstock)*

while there's plenty of white clapboard houses with matching picket fences and riverboats straight out of the pages of Mark Twain, there are also industrial smokestacks and urban sprawl; you get the full picture on this trip.

The route starts in the interesting twin cities of Minneapolis and St Pauls, then wends its way down some of the more scenic stretches to La Crosse; then Galena; Davenport; Hannibal (Mark Twain's boyhood home); St Louis; Memphis (Elvis and great food) and then on to Vicksburg (for Civil War history) and Baton Rouge, before arriving at New Orleans – the 'Big Easy' – just the place to celebrate the end of an epic road trip.

PLANNING NOTES

Start and finish: Minneapolis to New Orleans.
Distance: 1,500 miles (2,400km).
Time needed: Two weeks would work, but it really depends on what you want to see and do, and this trip could be both longer and shorter. Get planning!
When to go: September is said to be the best time to drive the GRR, largely because you have the start of the glorious autumn colours in the north while down south the humid summer will have come to an end but the weather will still be good. Winter is cold and snowy in the north.
Vehicle: Hire car; though this is likely to incur a drop-off fee.

Beware of: Don't expect bucolic vistas and Huckleberry Finn all the way down; there will be some grittier areas, too – if you're seeing all of America, you're seeing *all* of America.
Detours, extensions and variations: A trip from Minneapolis to Lake Itasca State Park will take you to the headwaters. This means you will be able to say you've truly travelled the course of the Mississipi; where you will also experience some marvelous scenery.
Further information: There's a navigation app and lots of other info available on experiencemississippiriver.com.

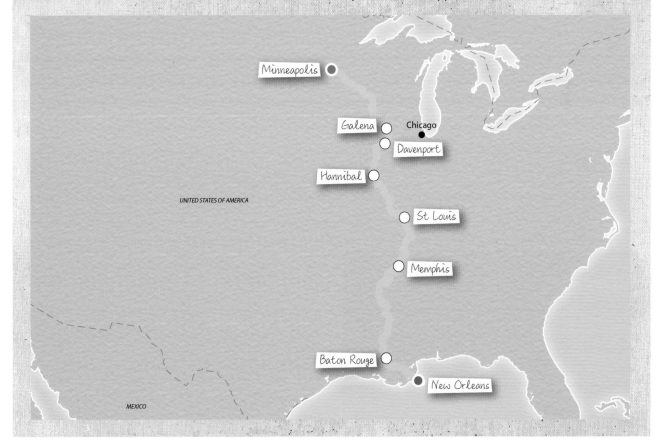

Two great drives can add up to one awesome road trip. The Skyline Drive and the Blue Ridge Parkway, which run down the spine of the southern Appalachians, are the perfect example of this. Combined, they stretch for 574 miles (925km) with plenty to explore along the route, while they're also within a day's drive of a number of US population centres, with Washington DC just 70 miles (113km) and one-and-a-half to two hours to the start of Skyline near Front Royal, while Cherokee, close to the southern end of the Blue Ridge Parkway, is about 170 miles (275km) and three hours from Charlotte.

Taking it from the top, the 105 mile (170km) Skyline Drive runs the length of the Shenandoah National Park in the Blue Ridge Mountains of Virginia. There's not a toll as such, but

▲ **The Linn Cove Viaduct on the Blue Ridge Parkway.** *(Shutterstock)*

rather a reasonable park entry fee – note that on occasion the drive can close due to snow while in the winter months it's shut overnight so rangers can control illegal hunting. These same rangers also strictly enforce the 35mph (56km/h) speed limit, which is in place to protect the wild turkey, deer and black bears that are part of the reason you're driving the route in the first place. So, this is not a place for a blat then. Rather, it's about enjoying the ride, enjoying unspoilt backwoods America, and enjoying the view – there is plenty to look at with some 75 viewpoints along the way.

Like the Skyline, the Blue Ridge Parkway is also a purpose-built scenic drive – a job creation scheme from the 1930s which was only fully completed in 1987 – and it also has a strict speed limit, which never exceeds 45mph (72km/h). The 469 mile (755km) route runs from the end of the Skyline Drive in Virginia at Rockfish Gap to the Great Smoky Mountains National Park near Cherokee in North Carolina. Unlike the Skyline, you don't need to pay to use it.

And use it you should, if you want to experience a lost

◀ **Mother bear and her cubs on the Skyline Drive – wildlife on the road is one of the reasons there's a strictly enforced speed limit.** *(Shutterstock)*

world of rustic log cabins, twanging bluegrass music and tales of moonshine. There's plenty to do along its length, too, with over a hundred hiking trails, plus kayaking and canoeing. This route is great for an RV, or simply camping under canvas, while there are also cabins to rent.

If you want to turn this into a good, long loop then this is possible by driving from Charlotte back to Washington, maybe stopping at historic Richmond and checking out the 23 mile (37km) Colonial Parkway, which runs from Jamestown to Yorktown, on the way.

PLANNING NOTES

Start and finish: Front Royal to Great Smoky Mountains National Park.
Distance: 574 miles (925km).
Time needed: You could do it in a few days if it's just a drive, but this area offers so much more and many will spend a week on the Blue Ridge Parkway alone.
When to go: Parts of both roads can close in the winter but conditions can be easily checked on their informative websites (see Further information). The autumn is very popular because of the riotous colours of the foliage, while traffic can be heavy in summer and on weekends. But then if you're in a rush you shouldn't really be on these roads.

Vehicle: Great for a camper or RV trip.
Beware of: Stops for provisions and fuel are few and far between, so fill up and stock up before hitting the road – though it is possible to drive off the ridge and find gas stations and shops at the access/exit point intersections with the regular highway.
Detours, extensions and variations: Famous with bikers and performance driving enthusiasts, the Tail of the Dragon is a tight and twisting antidote to the sedate nature of the main drives; head for Deals Gap on the Tennessee and North Carolina state line.
Further information: visitskylinedrive.org / www.blueridgeparkway.org.

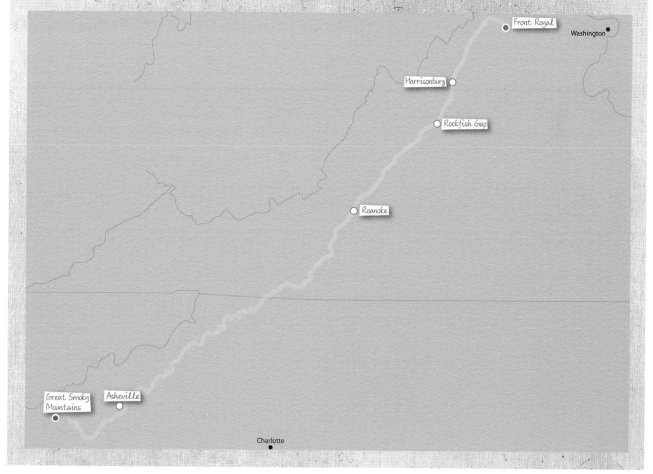

The 106 mile (170km) Overseas Highway is the closest you'll get to going on a Caribbean cruise by car. It's the southernmost section of A1A, the Florida coast road, and of US Route 1 – which runs 2,369 miles (3,813km) north to the Canadian border at Fort Kent in Maine, another excellent road trip to consider. On the Overseas Highway the road connects a string of keys – small islands – that sweep from the tip of Florida in a necklace of emerald beads strung together by a succession of low bridges that sometimes almost seem to float across the crystal clear sea between the Gulf of Mexico and the Atlantic Ocean – there are 84 bridges in all, including the impressive Seven Mile Bridge.

Once at Key West at the very tip of the USA, closer to Cuba than mainland Florida, you'll have to double-back to Key Largo to continue north through Miami, but that's no bad thing as this is a driving experience like no other, while you can always save some of the many sights for the return leg.

Beyond Miami, and the pastel-painted Art Deco buildings of South Beach, A1A will take you to Fort Lauderdale ('the Venice of America' with its canals, but also great beaches and museums) and on to affluent Palm Beach – but it's worth noting here that in towns buildings will often block the

▼ **The Seven Mile Bridge is part of the Overseas Highway that links the individual islands of the Florida Keys.** *(Shutterstock)*

▶ **Classic architecture meets classic car in Miami.**
(Patrick Farrell for Visit Florida)

sea view along the length of A1A and it's by no means one long esplanade.

After Palm Beach the road passes just west of Cape Canaveral and the John F Kennedy Space Center – it goes without saying this is a must-do – before heading on to Daytona Beach; visit at the start of the year and you *might* be able to get a ticket to NASCAR's most famous race, the Daytona 500, but failing that there's always the Daytona 24 Hours endurance race. You can also drive on the beach at Daytona, in the wheel-tracks of early land speed record breakers, but there's a strict speed limit.

The road then continues to trace the shore north to Amelia Island just south of Georgia with interesting towns like St Augustine, the oldest continuously inhabited city in North America, and wildlife viewing opportunities at the Guana Tolomato Matanzas National Estuarine Research Reserve, home to dolphins, manatees, sea turtles, American alligators and river otters. A1A takes on an interesting causeway-like character in this area, with the Atlantic to the right and the Guana River to the left, it's almost as surreal as when it began way out at sea connecting the dots of the Florida Keys.

PLANNING NOTES

Start and finish: Key West to Fernandina Beach, Amelia Island.

Distance: 600 miles (966km) – Orlando and Miami airports are within half a day's drive of the start and end points of this trip.

Time needed: This could be done in a week or a little more, but while distances are short there's a lot to see and do and many other attractions are close by, so to speed things up a little it might be worth taking to US-1 sometimes, or there's always the I-95 if you really want to make headway.

When to go: Winter is the best time to visit Florida south of Orlando, though it will be busy and prices might reflect this – it's also the low season for the north of the state, and although the sea might be cold it's still warmer than many places at this time of the year. Hurricanes are rare but the season is at its peak in August and September.

Vehicle: It can make sense to look at a fly-drive deal where you will get a discount on your car hire when you book your plane ticket – it's not unknown for the car to even come free with some flights.

Beware of: Florida once had a reputation for carjacking, but it's much safer now; at the time of writing car crime was at its lowest level since 1971. Still, use common sense. If someone drives into you then proceed to a well-lit spot with lots of people around before stopping, if you can, for instance.

Detours, extensions and variations: The Everglades National Park is famous for its alligators but it's also great for kayaking and hiking and is within easy reach of the A1A between Key Largo and Miami.

Fernandina Beach
St Augustine
Daytona Beach
Cape Canaveral
Palm Beach
Fort Lauderdale
Miami
Key Largo
Key West

Chapter 4

OCEANIA

From the sublime desert drives of Australia to the winding ways of New Zealand, Oceania is road trip nirvana. On its own, Australia is about never-ending, parched treeless straights, trails for 4x4s that are the perfect adventure and tropical drives along glistening coastlines. But its smaller neighbour New Zealand – though Kiwis will rightly point out it's over 2,500 miles (4,000km) away – can certainly rival it when it comes to road trip options, with rugged coastal routes and fantastic loops which perfectly blend culture, wildlife and scenery. And let's not forget the Pacific Islands. For the road trip driver, then, Oceania offers so much more than merely ocean.

▶ Outback driving in Western Australia. *(Tourism Australia)*

With very little in the way of towns to stop in along the way, a well-equipped campervan is just the thing when it comes to crossing Australia from south to north.

It's quite something to have a street named after you, but to have a 1,740 mile (2,800km) road – traversing what is, in effect, an entire continent – bear your name takes some doing. John McDouall Stuart did some doing. In 1861–62 Stuart, along with his nine-man team, became the first European to cross Australia from south to north, after a few unsuccessful previous attempts that were blighted by the inhospitable conditions and sometimes inhospitable indigenous people.

▼ Road trains are the kings of the Stuart Highway and you need to take care when overtaking them. *(Bresmedia)*

▼ This VW Crafter campervan proved to be the perfect vehicle in which to cross Australia from bottom to top. *(Bresmedia)*

Our journey across Australia south to north, Up the Guts as I've heard this trip called – though the road is more commonly referred to as The Track – was a little less heroic. But it's worth mentioning here that although the dangers and hardships are nothing compared to what Stuart and his men had to put up with, this is not a trip that should be taken lightly. The desert is big, and you are small, and you need to make sure – above all else – you take more water than you feel you're likely to need, and then a drop more. Same goes for fuel.

There are petrol stations along the entire route, but the gaps between them can be large – around about 125 miles (200km) – and you can't guarantee the fuel truck's always delivered. So, as always, but more so here, fuel up whenever you can. There are few towns, too, and some are tiny, so bear that in mind when thinking about provisions and accommodation. In short, this one needs a bit of planning.

We used a campervan for the journey, which makes sense when there's so much perfect wilderness to cross and so few towns to stay in. These are part and parcel of road trips in Oz and NZ, and there are plenty of companies offering very well-equipped vehicles. The only trouble we had with it, ironically enough, seemed to be because of fuel. We missed one stop, as we thought we had plenty, but the next station was out of diesel, and we had a 125 mile (200km) drive to the one beyond it. Thankfully, we were able to top

▼ The van was equipped with a fold-out barbie – essential equipment in Oz. *(Bresmedia)*

BY THE WAY ...

Aliens

This strange-looking creature (the one on the left) can be found at Wycliffe Well on the Stuart Highway. You'd probably stop here anyway, because that's what you do on The Track if there's a fuel station and roadhouse, but the little green aliens are an added attraction. Wycliffe Well is the self-proclaimed UFO capital of Australia. UFO sightings started in the Second World War, though people have claimed to have seen things – or not identified things, if you think about it – on many occasions since and still do. Apparently, the restaurant at the settlement has a huge range of beers, 300-plus ... I'm not saying there's a connection, you understand.

up at that single-pump station, but this seemed to be the cause of this one and only mechanical malady – well, sort of – when the engine warning light started flashing. I thought it might be iffy fuel, and sure enough on filling up the next day the worrying flashing stopped, so maybe it was. A nothing thing, perhaps, but in the middle of a desert with very few other vehicles around something like a pulsing orange light seems a little more sinister than it might on the M25.

We were actually well into our trip by the time of this little drama. We had started in Adelaide and driven to the Flinders Ranges for a spot of hiking to begin with, then picked up the Stuart Highway at its start at Port Augusta before spending a night in the surreal little opal mining town – and *Mad Max* film location – of Coober Pedy. From there it was a beautiful dawn start – there were a few of these – with a blood-orange sun lighting the way to Uluru. Kings Canyon, then Alice Springs were next, then a stop in the middle of nowhere (quite literally) before Katherine, followed by a detour off the Stuart Highway to Kakadu, and then on to the finishing line in Darwin, right at the top of Australia.

The flavour of this journey really changed once we were north of Port Augusta and properly on to the Stuart Highway. It was almost as if we'd strayed over that faint line between journey and adventure. Others must have thought the same, because just about everyone we met coming in the other direction – very few after a while – waved comradely or saluted by raising a few fingers off the wheel, an indication

▼ **Unmistakeable and unmissable – Uluru looking moody.**
(Bresmedia)

that we were sharing more than a road, more of an experience. Or maybe they were just friendly? Either way, this only stopped in the touristy bits, like Uluru.

That said, despite the lack of friendly waves, Uluru – or Ayers Rock if you like – was special. It's almost as if the rock is alive, as if it breathes. No doubt it's all about the way the light plays upon the surface of this 863m (2,830ft) monolith, rather than ancient spirits, but mystic or not it's very, very impressive.

There are a number of ways to experience the Rock, and walking around it is perhaps the simplest and best. People were still climbing it when we were there, but this was banned quite recently, mainly because it's such a sacred site to the indigenous people, the same as having tourists climb St Paul's in a way, but also because it's steep and can be slippery and people kept falling off … as would be the case with St Paul's, no doubt.

The drive to Uluru from Coober Pedy was the longest of the entire journey, at 465 miles (750km). That's probably pushing it a bit, but while there's a place called Marla on the map, in reality it's nothing more than a roadhouse and a scatter of streets (population 100), and there's not much to stop for. With a camper, of course, we could have stayed the night by the side of the road, preferably at one of the rest stops that are spaced out along the length of the Stuart Highway. But then again, there's a lot of ground to cover on this trip, and sometimes you just have to get on with it and drive.

But with days on the road as long as that one you really do need to make sure you factor in a bit of time for some activity beyond steering and accelerating – actually, there's not even much of that on the Stuart Highway. With this in mind there's a great hike around the rim of Kings Canyon which is well worth doing, while kayaking at Katherine Gorge is amazing. Get there early, for when the kayak hire shed opens its doors, and you can have the place to yourself. Very special.

There's also another highly recommended detour just north of Katherine; Edith Falls. There's a lovely lake here, a glorious spot for a morning swim. There's also a sign that says you should not go in the water between 8pm and 7am, as that's when the crocodiles feed. It was just gone 8am when we went in, and only then did I consider whether crocs ever had their equivalent of a midnight snack.

Crocodiles became a bit of a theme for the next day or so. North of Edith Falls we took a dogleg off the Stuart Highway to visit Kakadu National Park, which covers a huge area encompassing everything from mangrove fringed wetlands to sandstone escarpments and forest, with some

◄ **Kings Canyon is the perfect place to stretch your legs after a long day on the long road.** *(Tourism Australia/Tourism NT)*

BY THE WAY ...

Dead marsupials

Parked up one evening, our first in the camper at Wilpena Pound on our south to north trip across Australia, we found this kangaroo with a joey in her pouch, just metres from the van. After this initial encounter we thought we would see hundreds of 'roos on this trip, but we never saw another one. Not a live one anyway. I'm not sure why we started counting dead kangaroos – or maybe wallabies, as it's hard to tell when they're flattened – but by the end of the trip in Darwin the tally was up to 52. To be fair, we did see a few live wallabies; one bounced right in front of us on the road to Edith Falls, while another pair were practising their mixed martial arts at Katherine Gorge. We also sampled a beer called Kangaroo Pale Ale. It was hoppy.

▶ **Saltwater crocodile munching on his salad starters in Kakadu.** *(Bresmedia)*

fascinating ancient rock art to look at, too. It also has salties.

We saw plenty of these estuarine or saltwater crocs – the more dangerous type, which reach around 6m (20ft) in length – on a boat trip. The guide on the boat had to go through the spiel on life jackets and so on, though she did add that should the boat go down it would make no difference anyway as the crocs would get you soon enough. That's the thing about Australia, is there any other place in the world with so many creatures that can actually kill you?

Mind you, you're *very* unlikely to be killed by a croc, shark, snake, spider or jellyfish. More likely is a run-in with a kangaroo if you're driving after dark. Anyway, when it comes to the annoyance factor then after a little while you'll gladly take crocs over the damned flies! It took days after returning home before I got out of the habit of waving my hands around my face and head. We had come prepared, with head nets – available from any camping shop – which helped a bit, but be warned, even the emptiest parts of Australia are full of flies.

We were still sad to see the end of those empty parts, though. Darwin's an interesting and friendly city, and quite small, and Adelaide is lovely – worth a visit for the Central Market alone – but they seem like throbbing Tokyos in comparison with the close to 1,860 mile (3,000km) void

▶ **There are a lot of flies in outback Australia.** *(Bresmedia)*

▲ **One of the roadside attractions is the Devils Marbles; just a couple of them are shown here.** *(Tourism Australia)*

between them. It was especially weird having to deal with traffic again in Darwin after so much emptiness, and we even managed to get lost trying to find the hire depot.

That's pretty hard to do on the rest of this trip, as it's basically one long road. The driving is, then, pretty easy and the main challenge is not to drift off. You need to be aware of crosswinds, though, in a high campervan, especially after overtaking road trains – the ludicrously long three- and four-trailer trucks.

As for the view out of the window, the first part was mostly spinifex and dust and the odd salt pan glaring in the sun, and then it was rocky and hilly with lots of dried-out creeks around Alice Springs; further north was the Devils Marbles (a curious scatter of huge boulders); then it grew ever more verdant before Katherine (with lots of termite mounds); and greener still – tropical now – towards Kakadu and on to Darwin. Incidentally, the route is often referred to as The Track because until 1980 north of Alice that's what much of it was, but the entire way from bottom to top is now paved.

Our route wasn't the pure Stuart Highway, but it seems a shame to miss out on the crocs at Kakadu and on the wonders of Uluru when you're – almost – passing right by, and both were highlights of our trip. Yet while these were undoubtedly memorable, the most enjoyable aspect of this journey was simply driving through mile after mile of desert. Some find this monotonous, but there's something about this sort of road trip that is hugely meditative. Being in a desert gives you a unique perspective on your place in the world, in terms of both space and time, and just how infinitesimally tiny that slight sliver of existence is. The icing sugar scatter of stars across the clear outback sky at night then reminds you of this. It should be depressing, but it's not; it's life affirming, a prompt to make the most of it all. To keep driving on…

◀ **Clear night sky over Uluru.** *(Sean Scott/Tourism NT)*

PLANNING NOTES

Start and finish: Adelaide to Darwin.

Distance: 2,610 miles (4,200km) – that's for this entire trip. The Stuart Highway is 1,760 miles (2,834km) while Adelaide to Darwin is 1,880 miles (3,026km).

Time needed: At least a fortnight to do this trip justice.

When to go: It gets very hot in the Red Centre of Australia in the summer. We went in September, which was ideal.

Vehicle: A camper is perfect for this, but drop-off charges at Darwin are steep.

Beware of: Fuel is the big issue; fill up at every opportunity and take lots of water. Watch out for animals in the road, especially at dawn and dusk, and stop every few hours – to soak up the silence and also to help you avoid drifting off, as a long road can be mesmeric. In the summer, extreme heat can be a problem for both cars and drivers.

Detours, extensions and variations: If you've a 4x4 the Mereenie Loop Road, 112 miles (180km) out of Kings Canyon Resort, is a great little expedition, though this will require a permit.

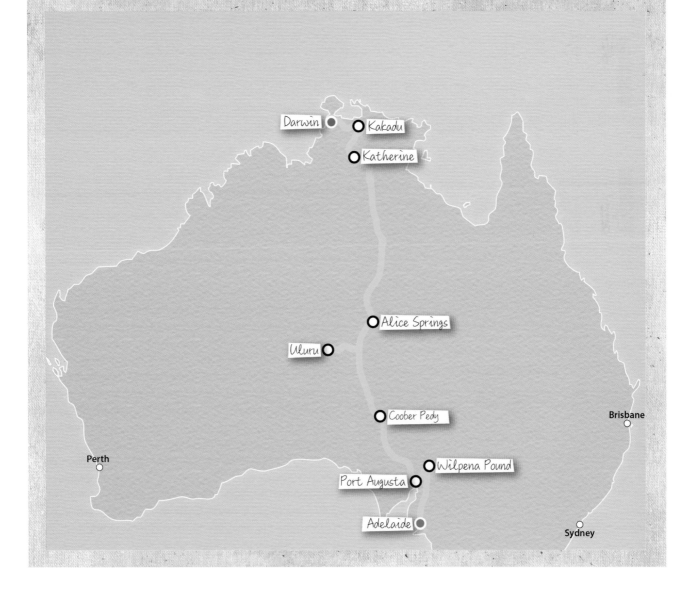

▲ **The Twelve Apostles with the Great Ocean Road wending its way along the clifftop.** *(Visit Victoria/Roberto Seba)*

It might be argued, and it has been, that Australia came of age during the First World War. Soldiers went to war as British, came back as Australian. But many stayed, too, buried in the heart-achingly sprawling cemeteries of Gallipoli and the Western Front.

But their country did not forget them, and how better for a young nation to commemorate its dead than with a road which would help it grow? The Great Ocean Road was not only meant as a memorial to the fallen, though, it was also a job creation scheme, with many returning soldiers working on it in conditions that may well have reminded them of Anzac Cove; living in tents and toiling with picks and shovels, while also exposed to not a little danger. But there was some light relief in 1924 when the SS *Casino* ran aground at Kennett River and the crew had to chuck 500 barrels of beer overboard to get it to re-float. There wasn't much work done in the following week.

These days, the longest war memorial in the world is a fitting tribute to both the fallen and to the men who built it. Starting in Torquay and unravelling in a series of twists and turns, it's a 150 mile (243km), mostly coastal drive along the B100 to Allansford. But to make a road trip of it you really need to put it into its wider geographical context,

◀ **Taking to the surf in Torquay after a day's driving on the Great Ocean Road.** *(Visit Victoria/Robert Blackman)*

starting from and then looping back to the marvellous city of Melbourne. An ideal itinerary might be this 412 mile (664km) trip, which can be comfortably completed in three days.

Day one takes you to Apollo Bay via Torquay – which is more *Point Break* than *Fawlty Towers*, a true surfer's paradise – and then Kennet River and its koalas. There's more wildlife and lush rainforest at nearby Otway National Park, before overnighting at Apollo Bay.

Day two is all about the main event on this drive, the much-photographed Twelve Apostles – though the sea has eroded their faith and there's just eight of these stone stacks jutting out of the Bass Strait now, the tallest of which is about 50m (164ft) high. There's also wildlife at Tower Hill State Game Reserve, where kangaroos, koalas and emus can be seen in the bowl of an extinct volcano, before staying the night at the picturesque fishing village and one-time whaling settlement of Port Fairy, which is beyond Allansford but worth the extra few miles.

Day three is the loop inland and back to Melbourne via Colac, passing through places known for gourmet food, where you can also stock up on some excellent craft beer. Is there a better way to finish a road trip?

PLANNING NOTES

Start and finish: Melbourne.
Distance: Suggested loop 419 miles (675km); Great Ocean Road: 151 miles (243km).
Time needed: Three days and two nights, but you could very easily spend a bit more time on this.
Vehicle: Melbourne is well-served with car rental companies.
When to go: The road's open all year but if you're on the lookout for whales then they'll be blowing between May and September.

Beware of: Erosion is a problem and rockfalls and landslides are not unknown, and if you're driving in Melbourne then familiarise yourself with the unusual rules for sharing the streets with its trams.
Detours, extensions and variations: Carrying on along the coast to Adelaide is a popular trip, or why not extend the loop and drive the Great Southern Touring Route, which heads north to Dunkeld and Halls Gap to visit the Grampians National Park and the old goldfields?

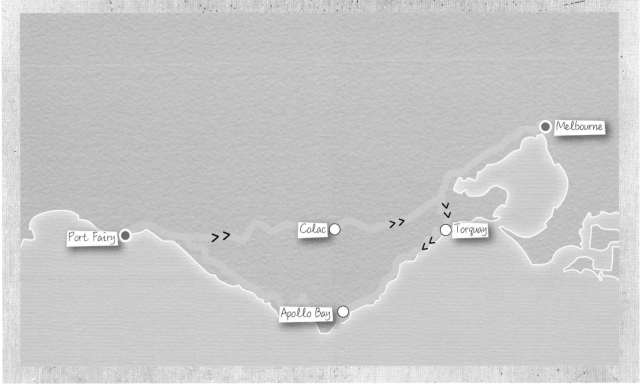

▲ A 1973 Chrysler Valiant Charger E48 turns in to a dusty apex on the Sideling stage during the 2018 Targa Tasmania. *(Angryman Photography/ targa.com.au)*

▼ Scenery is spectacular in Tasmania; this is Lake Dove and Cradle Mountain. *(Tourism Tasmania and Dominic Zeng)*

Even if you're not so interested in motorsport the fact that part of the reasoning for the inception of the Targa Tasmania in 1992 was to showcase some of the island's remarkable scenery means it's still a route that is well worth tracing.

That said, it's not as simple as just following a road, as despite the Targa name – taken from the famous Targa Florio in Sicily – the event itself is more of a tarmac stage rally than a road race. But you can get a flavour of it by splicing a few of the best bits together, and if you like a good drive then classic stages such as The Sideling, Cethana and Mount Arrowsmith should not be missed. The route outlined here should take you close enough to these, and thus act as a jumping-off point, while also linking up a number of Tasmanian beauty spots and places of interest.

This road trip starts and finishes in Hobart, sometimes described as a Sydney in miniature with a cool vibe and a great food scene – if you're there on a Saturday then don't miss the Salamanca Market. It then heads west to the interesting little old port of Strahan and from there it's on to Cradle Mountain-Lake St Clair National Park (the dramatically shaped mountain is a symbol of the island while there's great hiking to be had in the 1,000 square mile (1,612km^2) park); the Bay of Fires (with its sugar-white beaches and aquamarine sea); the Freycinet National Park (and the much-photographed Wineglass Bay) and then the Tasman Peninsula (with its Tasman National Park and the fascinating old penal settlement at Port Arthur). There's also much more to see and do, and many worthwhile places to stay, between all of these points.

Tasmania, the self-proclaimed 'curious island at the edge of the world', is a different type of wilderness to much of Australia, but there's plenty of it, including sub-tropical rainforests, lush plains, spectacular waterfalls (many to be found in national parks off the A10 to Strahan from Hobart) and stunning coastlines.

The island's also home to some of the best driving roads on the planet. If you doubt this, then bear in mind that after the first running of the Targa Tasmania, the driver of a Ford Mustang said it was 'one of the greatest driving experiences of my life'. That driver's name was Sir Stirling Moss.

PLANNING NOTES

Start and finish: Hobart.
Distance: 758 miles (1,220km).
Time needed: The Targa takes six days, but two weeks would be ideal for this.
Vehicle: There are plenty of rental options in Hobart for cars and campers while you can also bring a vehicle over on the ferry from Melbourne to Devonport in the north of the island.
When to go: The weather is notoriously changeable but February is the most stable month, while the rally takes place in April.

Beware of: If you're pushing then some of these roads are challenging, often fast yet also narrow, and watch out for blind crests. If you're taking it easy and the scenery's more your thing then try to buy a pass that covers all the parks, rather than paying for permits piecemeal. It works out much cheaper.
Detours, extensions and variations: Tasmania is fine road trip country and there are lots of possibilities, including heading south from Hobart and taking a ferry from Kettering to the wonderful Bruny Island.
Further info: targa.com.au

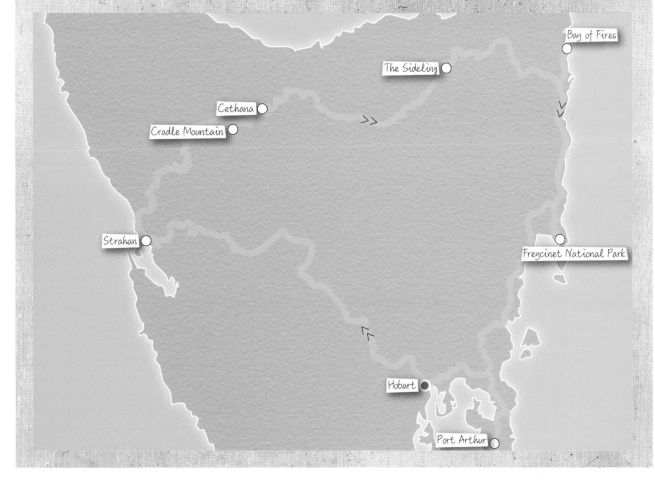

Sydney to Cairns; and a little bit more … The Pacific Coast route is an easy road trip, yet a long enough journey to gain a sense of satisfaction at the end of it. But there are also a few opportunities to make this a bit more than a long-distance fly-drive.

Over at least two weeks, north from Sydney (though it could, of course, be reversed) the route pretty much hugs the wonderful eastern coast of Australia. A popular schedule will read something like this. The first stop is Newcastle (Australia's second oldest city and a characterful

beach resort); through the wine country of the Hunter Valley to Pokolbin; Port Stephens (dolphin watching); Coffs Harbour; the chilled and Bohemian beach resort of Byron Bay; Queensland's Gold Coast (Surfers Paradise); Brisbane; Fraser Island (by ferry); Bundaberg; Rockhampton (via a detour west to the Cania Gorge National Park); Mackay; Townsville and finally Cairns.

If you make the trip over to Fraser Island and you're in a 4x4, you might want to look at driving the 75-Mile Beach Road, which skirts the eastern shore of the island. It is exactly what it says on the tin, a beach, yet it's also a road, with all the laws that this implies such as enforced speeding restrictions. It's a smooth drive but beware of dips and bumps, and keep an eye on the time, as you're not able to drive for two hours either side of high tide. They say the sand squeals as you drive over it, as might

▼ The Captain Cook Highway runs north from Cairns and is one of the world's best coastal drives in its own right – and just one of the reasons to keep on driving north.

(Tourism and Events Queensland)

you if you take a dip here as it's unsafe to swim because of the sharks.

Is that 'the little bit more'? Not exactly, I was thinking that perhaps an extension to Cape Tribulation (170 miles, or 280km, there-and-back from Cairns) might cap this trip off nicely, with the Great Barrier Reef on one side of the road and the 135-million-year-old Daintree Rainforest on the other as you drive. It includes the fabulous Captain Cook Highway and is tarmac all the way, except for the ferry across the crocodile-infested Daintree River. Now that's beginning to sound more like an adventure.

◀ **Kangaroos on the beach in Cape Hillsborough, Queensland: the only way you could make this picture more Australian would be to give one of them a boomerang.**
(Tourism and Events Queensland)

PLANNING NOTES

Start and finish: Sydney to Cape Tribulation.
Distance: 1,926 miles (3,100km).
Time needed: Two weeks is good, but you could also easily spend much longer, even a month, as there's plenty to do and see.
Vehicle: If it's just Sydney to Cairns you're looking at then pretty much anything will do. It's a popular trip so dropping off a hire car or camper will not be an unusual request.
When to go: The winter (June to September) is the best time to see Queensland, but then it can get a bit nippy in the south. On the other hand in the summer you get the monsoon rains in the north. Perhaps the shoulder seasons are the best options, then.
Beware of: Watch out for stuff in the sea on the tropical coast of Queensland; there are saltwater crocodiles on the beaches and jellyfish that have a sting that packs a punch a thousand times more potent than a tarantula. 'Stinger' season is between October and June. Note: some car hire firms will not allow travel to Fraser Island.
Detours, extensions and variations: If you crave a little more adventure and have a 4x4 then take the Bloomfield Track even further north.

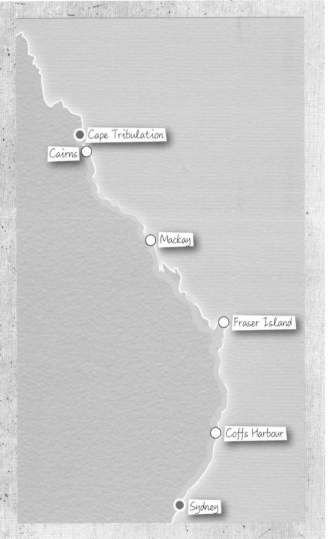

▲ The main problem with a Fiji road trip is prising yourself off the beach; this stretch of paradise is on the Coral Coast that the Queens Highway traces. *(Shutterstock)*

▼ The main roads in Fiji are mostly in pretty good condition. *(Shutterstock)*

If you're a rugby fan you might have sometimes wondered just how a tiny island nation like Fiji is so good at the game, especially sevens – it won gold at the 2016 Olympics. I might have the answer, for when I was there, admittedly some time ago now, the kids were playing without boots – now that's sure to hone your handling skills.

You won't need much in the way of handling skills when it comes to driving in Fiji, though; the roads are quiet and the driving is easy, while it's quite hard to get lost if you're following the edge of an island, it's just a matter of keeping the sea on the right.

The largest island in the Fijian archipelago is Viti Levu, and it's possible to drive right around it, making use of the well-known Queens Road in the south and the Kings Road in the north, with dense jungle and majestic mountains to look at on one side of the road, travel brochure cover beaches pinned in place with sloping palm trees on the other.

The Queens Road runs from Nadi (pronounced Nandi) to the capital, Suva – the international airport is at Nadi so it's a natural start and finish point for this trip. The road runs along the coral coast, where a reef protects some of the best beaches in the world, lapped by deep blue and aquamarine sea. It really is a picture-postcard paradise, but if you stop at just one of the beaches, then make it Natadola. Beyond this is Pacific Harbour, a centre for adventure activities such as swimming with sharks and jet skiing, and then Suva, which is the only real city in Fiji and worth a stopover to check out its colonial architecture and to sample the spicy Indo-Fijian cuisine. The rainforest at Colo-i-Suva Forest Park is worth a visit, too, with its native mahogany trees, waterfalls and pools for swimming in (it's just 15 miles, or 25km, north of Suva).

Driving on to the north of the island, scuba divers will enjoy a stop at Bligh Water, while strung along the Kings Road there are interesting villages and small towns like Tavua and Ba, where you can get a feel for the real Fiji. Oh, and if you want to play a bit of rugby while on the island, don't bother taking your boots.

PLANNING NOTES

Start and finish: Nadi.
Distance: 311 miles (500km).
Time needed: Four to seven days.
Vehicle: Car hire is not too pricey and there's plenty of options at Nadi airport, though you can get better deals in town.
When to go: The dry season, between May and October, is best for the weather, but it can get very busy in June and July, so you might want to book ahead when it comes to accommodation.

Beware of: Off the coastal road the tracks are usually unsealed and can be badly rutted and even impassable after heavy rains, so a 4x4 is advisable if you're looking at exploring the interior. And watch out for cows and chickens on the road.
Detours, extensions and variations: Take the ferry from Natovi to the smaller island of Ovalau and visit the town of Levuka, Fiji's former capital and now a UNESCO World Heritage site.

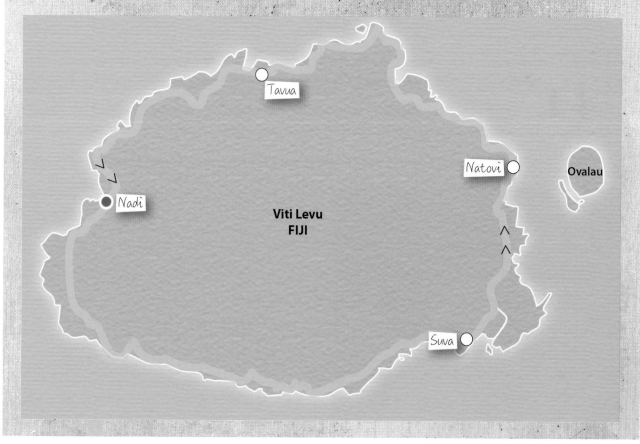

Auckland is at a pinch point in the centre of the North Island, so if it's a loop you're after then you will probably have to choose between heading north or south. We went south...

Heading along what's marketed as the Thermal Explorer Highway, the first part of this trip will give you an insight into Maori culture while also presenting you with an opportunity to have a crack at some of the adventure activities New Zealand's become famous for. But it's the hot stuff that this section of the route's been named for, as it passes through the country's geothermal region with its steaming geysers, bubbling pools and enchanting forests.

It's a great drive, often through distinctive rolling green scenery, and stops can be made at Hamilton (with its giant free flight aviary); Rotorua; Taupo (jet boat rides and kayaking) and Napier (which was rebuilt after an earthquake in 1931 and as a result it's now something of a time capsule for all things Art Deco).

▲ **The Champagne Pool in Rotorua: the area is a hotbed – pun intended – of geothermal activity.**
(Graeme Murray / Tourism New Zealand)

But it's Rotorua that's at the heart of this trip. The first thing that will hit you about this place is the smell. The crust of the planet is thin here and hydrogen sulphide leaks out through vents, filling the air with a rotten egg pong. You get used to it pretty quickly, though, and if not it's worth holding your nose for this is one of the world's most accessible geothermal areas, with 15m (50ft) geysers, bubbling mud, artist pallet-like mineral pools and steam venting everywhere. It's also a good place to learn a little about Maori culture, while there's plenty of bonkers adrenaline junkie stuff like zorbing, too.

After a stop in Napier, following the shoreline north will take you on to the Pacific Coast Highway, taking in the vineyards of Hawke's Bay and the remote East Cape region north-east of Gisborne – the highway runs for some 205 miles (330km) around this peninsula, hugging the coast all the way, so it's quite a long drive and you could cut straight across the peninsula if time is short.

A stop in either Tauranga or Mount Maunganui is then recommended, but to get back to the volcanic theme visit Hot Water Beach on the Coromandel Peninsula, where springs bubble up under the sand and you can dig your own hot bath to lie in on the beach. Oh, and don't forget to save time to explore Auckland, it's a great city.

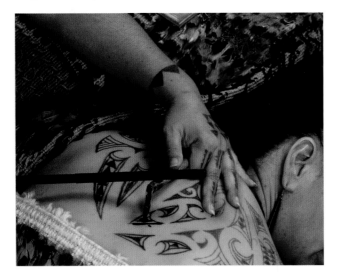

◄ **There are less painful souvenirs available in Rotorua – this is Moko, traditional Maori tattoos, which symbolically communicate messages about ancestry, prestige and social standing.** *(Tourism New Zealand)*

PLANNING NOTES

Start and finish: Auckland.

Distance: 944 miles (1,520km).

Time needed: As little as a week is possible (especially if you amputate the two peninsulas) but two weeks would be recommended to get the very best from this.

Vehicle: Hire from Auckland; a campervan would work well.

When to go: The best time for this loop is during the shoulder seasons, say October and November, or April; it's not so busy and it's easier to find accommodation.

May to September can be wet and colder, but it's still very doable.

Beware of: 'Sun-strike' is a real issue on winter mornings and late afternoons, where the low sun hitting the windscreen results in a blinding glare. Making sure your screen is clean will help, as will investing in a good pair of polarised sunglasses.

Detours, extensions and variations: Turn right at Hamilton and 30 miles (48km) along the SH23 is Raglan, a laid-back surfing town that's a great stop for a day or two.

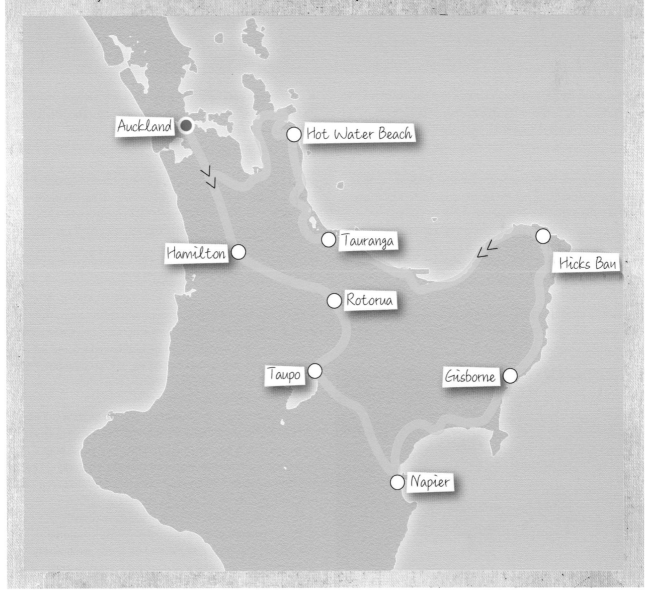

The speed is the surprising thing. I don't know why I was shocked to find you fall very quickly after jumping off a 43m (141ft) bridge – maybe it's because it can appear slow, even graceful, when you're looking on? Bungee jumping for paying punters actually originated in Queenstown, where I had a go a little while back. It's that sort of place. In fact, there are so many bucket-list ticking activities on hand you'll need a couple of biros when staying in this vibrant town, spectacularly set on the edge of Lake Wakatipu. But while there's plenty to see and do in the Queenstown area, venture further afield on the Southern Scenic Route and the rewards will amount to more than just a tick in a box.

▼ Finally, a good use for a cruise liner! This floating wedding cake really puts the magnificent Milford Sound in perspective. *(Rob Suisted / Tourism New Zealand)*

▲ Wild scenery and good driving roads are features of the Southern Scenic Route along its entire length. This stretch is near Otago. *(Graeme Murray / Tourism New Zealand)*

The Southern Scenic Route came about in the 1980s as a way of encouraging people to explore the bottom bit of New Zealand's South Island. The way is marked with a triangular sign showing a snaking S in a claret background and these dot a 380 mile (610km) route that describes a rough U shape from Queenstown to the city of Dunedin, or the other way round if you prefer.

There's a fine drive to Te Anau to begin with, set on the lake of the same name and a great base for hiking. This is also the jumping- off point for a day-drive to Milford Sound, an awe-inspiring 13 mile- (22km)-long fjord dominated by the otherworldly Mitre Peak. This really is a must-do – make sure you get out on the Sound in a kayak or on a boat trip – and the drive there is remarkable, at one point taking you through the rough-hewn Homer Tunnel.

From Te Anau the route skirts the eastern boundary of the picturesque Fiordland National Park and then traces the rugged south coast to Invercargill, then on to the dramatic Catlins Coast, with some of the wildest scenery in New Zealand plus swathes of natural forest and waterfalls such as the spectacular Pūrākaunui Falls. The official route finishes at Dunedin but it's quite easy to close the loop back to Queenstown.

By the way, there's also plenty of wildlife to see along the coast; including New Zealand fur seals, sea lions, dolphins and yellow-eyed penguins – you could use those biros to tick them off when you spot them.

PLANNING NOTES

Start and finish: Queenstown–Dunedin (or loop back to Queenstown).

Distance: 379 miles (610km), or 559 miles (900km) as a loop.

Time needed: Five days (could be fewer if you're in a rush).

Vehicle: Despite its small size, Queenstown has a decent number of car hire and campervan rental options, testament to its importance as a tourism hub.

When to go: If you're a skier or a snowboarder Queenstown's a great place to be in the winter, while the route outlined is usually okay to drive the year round.

Beware of: If the weather does turn snowy you might need snow chains to get to Milford Sound; keep an eye on the forecasts and take local advice. Make sure you fuel up whenever you have a chance; it's a remote part of the world.

Detours, extensions and variations: There are some great drives out of Queenstown, including the 42 mile (68km) Crown Range Road, the more direct and the far more exhilarating of two ways to Wanaka, and also the highest tarmacked pass in New Zealand (3,500ft, or 1,076m, at the top). Loop back the other way to make it a great day-drive.

If you're not a fan of desert driving then on its own the Eyre Highway may well seem like a road to nowhere, from nowhere – albeit a very, very, very, long road. It links South Australia with Western Australia and it crosses the Nullarbor Plain, an area of flat, pretty much treeless, arid terrain butting up against the Great Australian Bight coast, with the Great Victoria Desert to the north.

▼ **Not many desert drives offer whale spotting, but southern rights can be seen from the Head of the Bight, where these are pictured, at the right time of year.**
(South Australian Tourism Commission)

▲ **There's not a lot along the Eyre Highway but what there is can certainly dent your car.** *(Greg Snell)*

The road runs for 1,030 miles (1,660km) from Port Augusta to Norseman, crossing the state border near Eucla, and at its western end, between Balladonia and Caiguna, it is extremely flat and straight – the sixth longest straight road in the world, apparently. By the way, if you drive this highway and you wonder about the stripes that mark the edge of the road – here and on other straight sections of asphalt in Oz – these are the temporary landing strips used by the Royal Flying Doctor Service.

This is not quite your average desert drive, though, as the proximity of the sea means there's the chance to spot whales; and the Head of the Bight (a dramatic spot between Ceduna and Eucla) is a good place to watch southern right whales as they migrate along the coast between June and October.

Even with the whales it's a long drive with not much in the way of a narrative. But when you factor the Eyre Highway in as a part of a wider journey that connects the quaintly wonderful Adelaide and its very interesting surrounding area with the many, many delights of the southern part of Western Australia, then this is certainly a road trip that's worth doing.

PLANNING NOTES

Start and finish: Adelaide to Perth.
Distance: 1,678 miles (2,700km). Eyre Highway is 1,031 miles (1,660km).
Time needed: There's not much to stop for on the Eyre Highway, so three or four days would do it, but quite a bit longer if you want to see more of Adelaide and Perth and the many attractions around them.
Vehicle: Campervans, a great option due to the scarcity of good places to stay along the route, are available for hire in both Adelaide and Perth.
When to go: It gets very, very hot in the Australian summer. Winter is best for spotting whales at the Head of the Bight.

Beware of: Watch out for kangaroos, wild camels and emus in the road, especially at dawn and dusk – some of the 'roos in this area are simply huge. The other danger, as is the case on all long straight roads, is falling asleep at the wheel. Take breaks when you can. And carry plenty of water.
Detours, extensions and variations: If you're a golfer then you might want to pack your clubs and play a round at the Nullarbor Links, probably the longest golf course in the world, its 18 holes stretching 848 miles (1,365km) from Kalgoorlie to Ceduna (for more go to nullarborlinks.com).

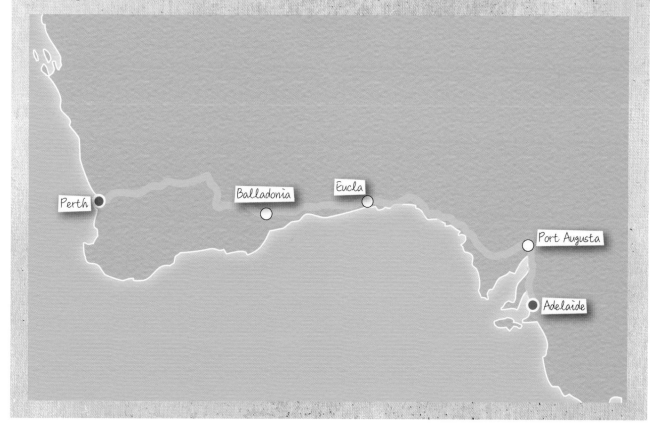

Billed as 'Australia's Adventure Drive', the Savannah Way is a 2,300 mile (3,700km) route that links 15 national parks and five World Heritage areas and, rather more dramatically, traverses Australia. There's an excellent website (see Planning notes) which is full of tips and hints and also breaks the route down into three parts which are cracking road trips or adventures in their own right:
Broome to Katherine; Katherine to Normanton; then Normanton to Cairns.

There are many options as to how you go about this trip, which means you can pick and choose the level of adventure. For example, between Broome and Katherine you could opt for the Gibb River Road, a legendary outback drive which stretches from Derby to Kununurra (410 miles, or 660km). It's a mix of tarmac and gravel, the latter graded at the end of the wet season every year, and while it can be tackled in a regular car a tough 4wd is definitely recommended. Corrugations are not unknown on this road, but it's worth the shaking to see Bells Creek Gorge and the stunning ancient aboriginal rock paintings at Tunnel Creek.

From Katherine to Normanton there's options for whether you're in a 2wd or a 4wd, and you'll need to plan your journey with this in mind – but make a detour and visit Lawn Hill Gorge in Boodjamulla National Park if you can, especially if you're packing a kayak.

The last stage, assuming you're travelling west to east, is

▼ **The Savannah Way in the Northern Territory; this is typical of some of the tracks along the route.** (Peter Eve/Tourism NT)

Normanton to Cairns. Sealed roads and more towns make this a little less of an adventure, but still a great road trip, and if you're keen to see the wilder parts then rest assured there are more than enough side roads and detours for the incurable explorer.

If you're planning on driving the entire Savannah Way then the operable word there is 'planning'. You really need to time it right, as some of the roads can take a while to recover from what's locally referred to as a 'big wet'. State and territory governments have advice lines and websites showing up-to-date road conditions and these are listed on the Savannah Way site.

▶ **It might be asphalt as you get towards Cairns but there are still hazards to watch out for.** *(Tourism & Events Queensland)*

PLANNING NOTES

Start and finish: Broome to Cairns (the map shows just one route option).

Distance: 2,300 miles (3,700km).

Time needed: There's no reason why you couldn't do one of the stages as a two-week holiday and three to four weeks for the whole thing is certainly doable – as ever, it depends on what you want to see and do.

Vehicle: Camper hire is a good option, but a 4wd is more sensible. The drop-off fees could be steep if you're hiring but both are available in Broome and Cairns.

When to go: Best to avoid the rains and the hottest months, so between May and October could be good.

Beware of: In some areas and national parks the roads can become impassable during the wet season, and they can close within half an hour of the start of a deluge in the tropics. There are some very remote stretches, too, so a satellite phone might make sense.

Detours, extensions and variations: There are a number of Savannah 'ways', so pick the best for you and your vehicle.

Further information: www.savannahway.com.au

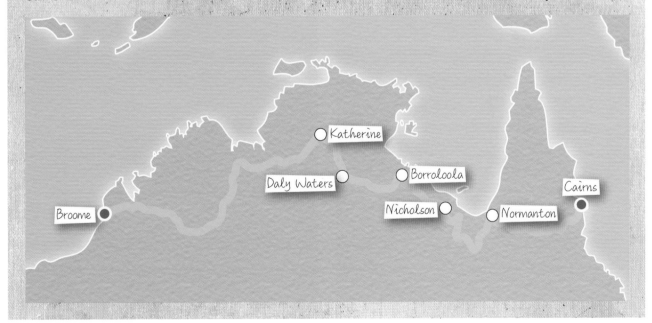

With a total length of around 9,000 miles (14,500km), Highway 1 is said to be the longest highway in the world, though in truth it's a network of roads. Some say the Pan-American Highway stretches further anyway, but that has a rather large lacuna – the very dicey Darién Gap. What can't be disputed, though, is that this is without doubt the longest *ring road* in the world.

Running roughly – very roughly in some places – around the edge of Australia, the Big Lap, as it's sometimes called, was created in the mid-'50s, and passes through all Australian states and territories, with the exception of the Australian Capital Territory. There's even an offshoot of it in Tasmania.

Because it's a ring road you can start wherever you want – it passes through all the state capitals – and as you might expect from a road that sees a lot of Australia, the road conditions are a little bit of everything, from multi-lane motorways to single-lane gravel tracks. It also includes iconic

drives such as the Great Ocean Road, the Eyre Highway and the trip up the Pacific coast that are detailed elsewhere in this chapter.

While this is not entirely a coastal route – there are some big shortcuts, particularly in the wild north of the country – it's not all desert, either. In fact, Highway 1 touches nearly all the inhabited areas of the country and also goes through swamps, scrubland, and tropical forests. If you want to really see Australia, then, this is the way.

But as you might imagine, this is not a trip that can be completed in a week. Many Australians sell up when they retire and take a few years to do this; the so-called Grey Nomads. That said, it needn't take that long, and in 2017 Team Highway 1 to Hell set a new record for the route – not including the Tasmania bit – of a staggering five days, 13 hours and 43 minutes, 'stopping only for fuel, food and urgent toilet breaks'.

▼ **While the Ring Road might not hug the coast all the way round, it certainly does along the Sea Cliff Bridge in New South Wales.** *(Tourism Wollongong)*

▼ **Australia's not all dusty tracks and coastal roads, and you're also sure to see some lush jungle while driving the Lap.** *(Tourism Queensland)*

PLANNING NOTES

Distance: 9,000 miles (14,500km).

Time needed: As much as a year or more, maybe as little as two months.

Vehicle: While a camper or RV would be ideal for the easy bits, a good 4x4 might be needed for the rougher stretches. Hiring a car for this might be possible – and you certainly won't have to worry about one-way drop-offs – but buying a vehicle in Oz would make more sense.

When to go: This depends on where you start and finish, and on whether you go clockwise or anti-clockwise. But wherever you start, if it's summer then head south, if it's winter, head north.

Beware of: All the usual hazards of an Australian road trip, as you'll be driving on all the Australian roads.

Detours and variations: Once you've finished you could always do a lap of honour!

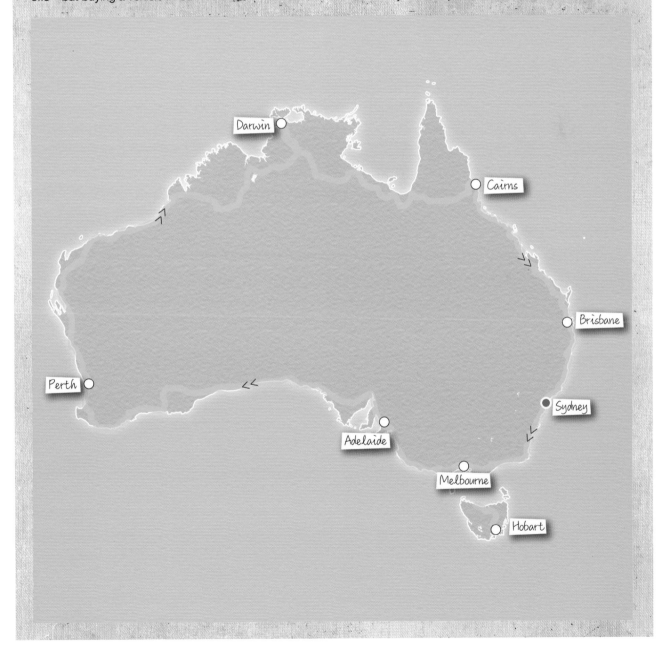

Chapter 5

AFRICA

Africa is a byword for adventure and the most exciting place for a road trip there is. But it's not all full-on expeditions and off-road driving and there's a trip to suit every budget and taste; from meandering through wineries and sleepy coastal towns in South Africa, to crossing the beautifully stark deserts of Namibia, or negotiating the twisting passes across the Atlas Mountains in Morocco. It's a vast continent of stunning coastlines, exotic forests and jaw-dropping acacia-studded plains that stretch further than the eye can see. Oh, and let's not forget the wildlife…

◀ **Driving through the desert, close to the Skeleton Coast in Namibia.** *(Bresmedia)*

As road trips go, 6,500km through five African countries in an overland-equipped 4x4 is perhaps on the extreme side, but with a little careful planning this is an adventure anyone can enjoy.

One moment we were alone in our wilderness campsite, except for a distant herd of elephants, grey battleships drifting on the slightly swishing sea of the silvery grass plain. The next we were confronted by three heavily armed men, appearing from nowhere, their camouflage making it seem as if the bush itself had suddenly come alive. But then that's Africa, always surprising…

We had been on this journey for a little while by then, so we were used to such surprises. It's what makes any road trip in Africa an adventure, even if you have planned it down to the last detail, and with this one that had certainly been the case.

▶ **This rather dirty elephant really took a dislike to us in Zimbabwe. There was no shifting her and we had to find another way around.** *(Bresmedia)*

▼ **The Nissan truck we hired was just the ticket for this trip.** *(Bresmedia)*

▲ **Home from home: the roof tent was easy to put up and the truck was packed with everything we needed to spend a night in the bush.** *(Bresmedia)*

▲ **Approaching Spitzkoppe: Namibian gravel roads are pretty good, but in a high vehicle like this you need to be careful in the corners.** *(Bresmedia)*

I had always wanted to drive the classic overland route, London to Cape Town. It's never quite been feasible, though. Either we've not had enough time, or more often we've not had enough money, or sometimes Africa's just had way too much politics. So we began to think of a way we might get a real taste of the continent without spending a small fortune, taking too much time off work, or getting shot. After hours poring over maps and weighing up pros and cons we decided on a four-week, 4,000 mile (6,500km) curl that took us from Johannesburg in South Africa, into Namibia, then Botswana, Zambia, Zimbabwe and finally Botswana again. The route itself was dictated by the pick-up and drop-off options with the hired truck, but it also took into account our desire to get a real flavour of Africa, encompassing as it did vast grasslands, deserts, mighty rivers and waterfalls. Not to mention some of the finest game parks this wonderful continent has to offer.

Originally we had plotted a course that would have included a big chunk of Mozambique, visiting Swaziland and then a return to Johannesburg, which traced a heart shape, and we thought of it as the Heart of Africa trip, but that would have taken a little bit too much time and money so in the end we had to cut it down. There was nothing half-hearted about what remained, though.

Forward planning for this was vital, as some of the best wilderness campsites in the depths of the game reserves need booking well in advance, while we also had a lot of ground to cover and we wanted to make the most of the

limited time. And yet, despite all the careful scheming, we were still forced to break the golden rule for driving in Africa on the very first day.

Driving at night in Africa is always a no-no, but we had massively underestimated the time it would take to go through all the paperwork and to be shown how to use the equipment – compressor, gas hob, roof tent etc. – on the Nissan truck, while the 370 mile (600km) or so drive to the edge of the Kalahari, from the depot in Johannesburg to Kuruman, took a lot longer than expected. I thought it an okay risk, for a one-off – this was South Africa, after all. But there were still dramas; there tend to be when some fellow road users don't use their lights. But on the upside there was also an awesome sunset to drive into; a sky of blue, black and gunmetal to one side; burning peach to the other, before all of it seemed to dissolve into purple smoke.

After a night in Kuruman we drove on into the Kalahari and we were soon off the asphalt, in South Africa's Kgalagadi Transfrontier Park (which also covers part of Botswana, hence the name). On entering we were advised to reduce our tyre pressures to 1.6bar (from 2.5bar at the front; 3bar, rear), because of the corrugations on the tracks. These were bad enough to shake a filling loose in places so as wonderful as the scenery and wildlife was in Kgalagadi, we were a little relieved to cross the border into Namibia, where the unpaved roads are very good indeed.

Not all of Namibia's roads are unpaved – there are long sections of tarmac main roads too – but many are, and

▲ **The wildlife is a little different on the Skeleton Coast; baby seal at Cape Cross.** *(Bresmedia)*

most are of a standard to make fairly rapid progress possible (though you need to be careful). But whatever the surface, the best thing about driving in Namibia is the emptiness. Crossing the Namib Desert to reach the sea at Walvis Bay we hardly saw another car, and the same was so on the

▼ **In the north of Namibia everything seems more African.** *(Bresmedia)*

magnificent drive up the Skeleton Coast to Terrace Bay. Before that we had approached the coast from the middle of the desert, where we'd camped at Spitzkoppe, and as we headed west in the bright morning sunshine a dark seam suddenly appeared on the distant horizon, growing into a black band between sand and sky as we came closer. We immediately thought we were heading into a sandstorm and so started to check the windows were shut tight. But then we realised it was not sand, but fog over the coast. As experiences go, driving through a desert in the fog takes some beating … but bursting out into the sunlight the other side comes close.

It's not all desert in Namibia, far from it. As you head north the character of the land – and even of the towns and villages – changes dramatically. From the Mururani Gate, a gap in the veterinary control fence on the road to Rundu, everything begins to feels more green, more 'African': there are far more trees, the population's much denser, while there's a big increase in the amount of cattle and donkeys on the roadside – and on the road.

Africa's been shaped by European politics, quite literally, and sometimes the borders are only there for Westerners, it seems. At Rundu the locals crossed the Kavango to visit Angola at will; many popping over to a funeral with beautiful singing well into the night while we were there. The Caprivi Strip is another example of European map drawing, a finger of Namibia, wedging open a narrow gap between Zambia and Botswana. It was the result of a deal between Britain and Germany (Namibia was a German colony up until the First World War), which included a land swap, in order to

BY THE WAY ...

Rust in peace

Namibia's Skeleton Coast gets its name from the whale and seal bones that once littered its shore, the detritus of the whaling industry, though some also insist it's because of the many ships that have been wrecked along it. Most of these wrecks have now been pounded by the unforgiving Atlantic to nothing more than splinters of wood and scabs of iron, and those that remain are difficult to get to, while improvements in technology means there are no modern wrecks. Except, that is, for the *Suiderkus*, a large trawler that ran aground on its maiden voyage in 1976. It is close to Henties Bay on the salt road – quite a way south of the official Skeleton Coast park – and easy to get to with a regular two-wheel drive car from Swakopmund, as we

did on an earlier trip. I've heard this wreck's beginning to disintegrate now though, and it won't be long before its resident cormorants will have to find a new home.

give Germany access to the Zambezi River. We drove along the Strip – to be honest a boring drive unless an elephant is on the road – stayed close to the border and then crossed into Botswana.

Our stay in Chobe was memorable. The armed men I mentioned at the start were actually a three-man Botswanan army patrol. I was cooking chilli on the single hob when they appeared and they chatted for a while. They were on anti-poaching duties (luckily I wasn't doing eggs), which made me wonder if the danger we faced was not so much from the lions we heard roaring in the night, but more the desperate

men who were after the tusks of our near neighbours. Those elephants came very close that night, while a herd of buffalo passed either side of the truck, too, which was quite an experience. As was crossing into Zambia.

This meant using the Kazungula Ferry to cross the Zambezi, the direct way from Botswana to Zambia. To get to the ferry you first need to drive past a queue of lorries that stretches for about a mile and maybe more. I'm glad we had

▼ **This Botswanan army anti-poaching patrol visited our camp in Chobe.** *(Bresmedia)*

BY THE WAY ...

No horns please

Unusual rocks are not uncommon in the magical Matopos Hills of Zimbabwe. But this boulder stood out because it was unnaturally close to the very edge of the narrow road we were driving along. It stood out more when it stood up ... It was a rhino, with a calf that had been hidden behind the boulder-like bulk of its prehistoric body. And we were not even in a game reserve. The mother rhino and child shuffled into the foliage, as can be seen in this hastily snapped picture, before we had time to worry about it charging us. Then we realised she actually had no horn. At first we wondered whether a poacher with a heart had just taken the horn and not the life of this magnificent creature, but then it became obvious that

it had been removed to make sure a poacher would not be interested. Extreme, and very sad, and just one approach to a problem that is not going away.

◀ **Victoria Falls from the Zambian side – a picture does no justice to the grandeur, the noise, or just how wet you get!** *(Bresmedia)*

been advised to drive past and not join the line, as I'm sure we'd still be there now otherwise. The ferry is just a single pontoon, with room for two trucks and a handful of cars, so no wonder the queue was so long. What's remarkable is that none of the lorry drivers seemed to mind us pushing ahead, and we were even waved to the front of the queues in the border and custom control offices.

On the other side of the river things were not quite so simple and we spent a few hours there, then left to visit the truly awesome Victoria Falls with the sound of rubber stamps still thudding in our ears. The next crossing, after using Livingstone as a base for some day drives in Zambia, was in to Zimbabwe, and we had been a bit worried about that one. Yet while it took a couple of hours, the process was efficient, and the officials were very friendly.

Friendly is actually the adjective that first comes to mind when I think of Zimbabwe. At the time we visited, Mugabe was still in power and some questioned the wisdom of even going there. I'm very pleased we did, though, as this is one of the most remarkable countries I've ever set foot in.

Much of the negative stuff we'd heard about Zimbabwe was to do with the police; there was a lot of talk about having to bribe your way through roadblocks and so on.

◀ **Looking for lions in the long grass with an armed ranger in Zimbabwe.** *(Bresmedia)*

We saw nothing of this. Okay, they are very active, there are checkpoints right the way down the road from Victoria Falls to Bulawayo, and they check everything; warning triangles, reversing lights, import documents, and so on (for more on this see The basics), but we never had any real issues.

A highlight of Zimbabwe was the hike in lion country in Hwange National Park. We didn't see any lions – though we have on walking safaris since and it's a thrill to encounter them on foot – but it was still hugely exciting. Our guide was a park ranger who had a rifle, an unpronounceable name and a wealth of great stories. My favourite was the one about the lion that had made a kill outside a park office building. A colleague of his switched on the light inside which startled the lion into jumping through the closed window. The floor was tiled and the lion, its claws wet with blood from its dinner, slipped and slid on the tiles and was unable to catch the petrified ranger. The ranger got to the gun rack and it didn't end well for the lion.

Our time in Zim' did end well, with a stay in the spellbinding Matopos Hills, before crossing once more into Botswana where we had a close encounter with a bunch of angry hippos while on a mokoro (dugout canoe) in the Okavango Delta. But that's another story. Then that's Africa, one story after another – and always another surprise waiting around the corner.

PLANNING NOTES

Start and finish: Johannesburg to Maun.
Distance: 4,040 miles (6,500km) – the route is actually around 3,800 miles (6,100km), the rest is driving around game parks and other excursions.
Time needed: Four weeks.
When to go: We went in May, which was fine, but it could be cold at night when camping.
Vehicle: Overland-equipped 4x4s such as the Nissan we used are available to rent throughout southern Africa, particularly in Namibia and South Africa.

Beware of: See the section on driving in Africa in 'On the road' in The basics chapter.
Detours, extensions and variations: If we had had a bit more time it might have been nice to loop back to Jo'burg, which would have saved a lot on the drop-off fee, but we couldn't quite make this work without missing some things we had deemed unmissable.

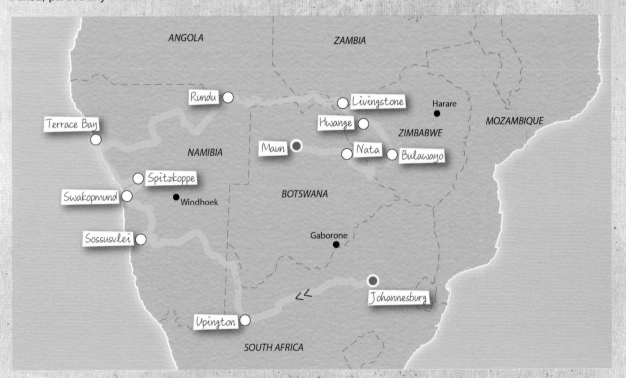

While the word 'garden' may not get the heart thumping, this is a great introduction to African road trips; with a huge range of topography and vegetation, wildlife aplenty, stunning coastal scenery and an impressive list of activities including hiking and kayaking. It is also a very popular and relatively cheap South African fly-drive package.

The Garden Route starts at Mossel Bay, but you're more likely to begin this drive in Cape Town. From there it might be worth thinking about heading for Stellenbosch before picking up Route 62, then hitting the Garden Route at Knysna. Cape Town is vibrant, colourful and exciting, and a trip up to the top of Table Mountain is not to be missed, while the historic university town of Stellenbosch is a great destination in its own right.

Route 62 is a quiet drive that takes in much of the area's wine country and is an alternative to the more southerly, and busier, N2 for getting to the start of the Garden Route. Highlights include tribal art and cultural tours, museums, hiking and 4x4 trails. Oh, and the vineyards, of course.

A common itinerary for the Garden Route itself would

▼ The Bloukrans Bridge on the Garden Route. *(Shutterstock)*

▶ The Garden Route is dotted with pleasant places like Knysa. *(South African Tourism)*

be to head south from Oudtshoorn (the Cango caves and ostriches) to Wilderness (lakes and natural lagoons); on to Knysna and then Plettenberg Bay, where you can explore the beaches or visit Tsitsikamma National Park with its indigenous forest, deep river gorges and waterfalls – the verdant and diverse vegetation in this area is the reason for the Garden Route's name.

Port Elizabeth, 'the friendly city', is next, and from here the fly-drive trips usually include a spot of big game watching – making this a true introduction to Africa – at the Eastern Cape Game Reserves, where there's the opportunity to spot the Big Five: lion, elephant, leopard, rhino and buffalo.

The drop-off will usually be at Port Elizabeth Airport, but it's easily possible to make this an interesting loop by returning to Cape Town via the N2 – having saved some sights from the outward leg – and then making a diversion that takes in the De Hoop Nature Reserve, Cape Agulhas – Africa's most southerly tip where the Atlantic Ocean meets the Indian Ocean – and Hermanus, for whale watching.

PLANNING NOTES

Start and finish: Cape Town to Port Elizabeth
(or return to Cape Town).

Distance: 516 miles (830km) to Port Elizabeth; 1,081
miles (1,740km) for the loop shown here.

Time needed: Two weeks to do the full trip, less if
you're dropping off in Port Elizabeth.

When to go: It can be wet and grey from August
to October, but on the other hand the area is
hugely popular during the SA summer months and
accommodation prices can be high as a result.

Vehicle: Hire car from Cape Town.

Beware of: Cape Town gets a bad press in terms of
the level of crime, but if you're sensible you will be
okay. That's not to say there's nothing in it and there
are very high levels of violent crime in the townships,
as is the case across South Africa, and those on the
Cape Flats should be avoided unless you have a guide
you trust.

Detours, extensions and variations: If you're after
more of a driving challenge then from Oudtshoorn head
north across the spectacular Swartberg Pass, a single-
lane gravel road that's justly considered one of the
most spectacular drives in the world.

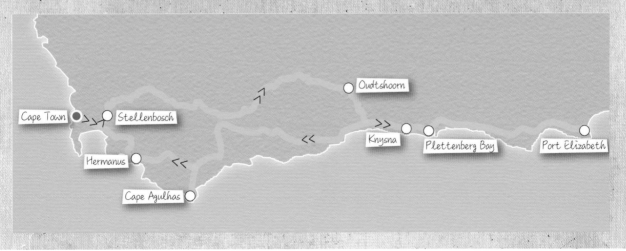

Long lens or upgrade to a 4x4? There was £400 in our budget for either option, but it would not cover both. In the end we chose zooming in on lions over zooming over rough tracks, but we never regretted this, for although many of the roads in Namibia are unsealed the quality is generally pretty good, and the VW Polo we hired proved to be up to the task.

That said, I've noticed that 2wd cars tend not to be offered so much with packages these days, but then whatever car you use you will have an amazing time in Namibia. It's a beautiful country and one of the most exciting road trip destinations there is.

The basic Namibian road trip starts at the capital, Windhoek (you'll need to book a table at Joe's Beer House, but don't miss it). From there it's a run down the paved R1, dodging the odd troop of baboons to remind you that yes you're really in Africa, before you hit the gravel and head for the tiny desert outpost of Solitaire, where there's a graveyard for old classic cars and a real roadhouse feel. There's fuel, too, and you should really fill up and get into the habit of doing so, as there's a lot of empty desert on this trip.

Most spend the first night at Sesriem, where you'll need to go easy on the ice cold Hansa if you're to enter the Sossusvlei National Park at dawn the next day. It's worth the early start, too, especially for photographs, as the majestic dunes are at their sharp-edged best in the morning light; don't miss Deadvlei with its petrified ancient trees, or the

◀ **This VW Polo was great fun in the Namibian desert.** *(Bresmedia)*

▼ **Petrified ancient trees in the surreal landscape of Deadvlei, which sits amidst the towering sand dunes of Sossusvlei National Park.** *(Bresmedia)*

short hike out to Hidden Vlei if you want to truly sense the sublime emptiness and quietude of the desert.

From Sossusvlei the drive to Swakopmund (like a Bavarian town on the wild African Atlantic coast) is amazing, through mountain passes and then crossing the empty desert for 60 miles (100km) or so to Walvis Bay – make a point of stopping to soak up the solitude and the silence for ten minutes. North of Swakopmund there's a nice section of the Skeleton Coast salt road and then desert track again to Khorixas (and the best kudu, eland or gemsbok you'll ever taste at Vingerklip Lodge). Etosha's next (a chance to see lion, elephant, giraffe, rhino and much more); and then back to Windhoek via, for us, Okonjima (for leopards and cheetahs). For packing a lot of Africa into a reasonably sized trip, nothing beats Namibia.

PLANNING NOTES

Start and finish: Windhoek.
Distance: 1,300 miles (2,100km).
Time needed: About ten days would be fine for the trip outlined here, with a two-night stop in Sesriem and three in Etosha.
When to go: We went in late May into June, which was great; late July until the end of October is the busiest time. Booking ahead is advisable at most times of the year.

Vehicle: Hire car or 4x4 from Windhoek Airport.
Beware of: It's easy to let the speed climb too high on the very good loose surface roads in Namibia, and people do get caught out. Also, fill up when you can.
Detours, extensions and variations: Head further south and there's the eerie ghost town at Kolmanskop to explore and the awesome Fish River Canyon to hike.

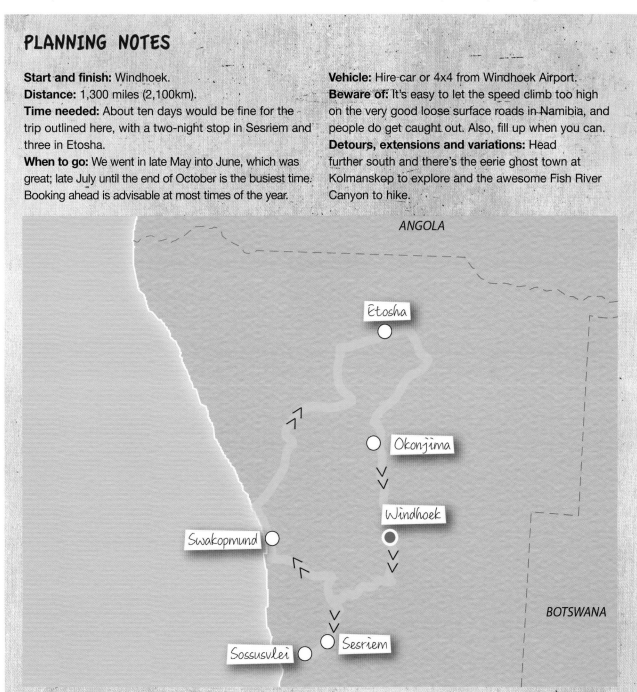

▲ **The Tizi n' Test pass can be challenging; but that just makes it more of an adventure.** *(Shutterstock)*

The High Atlas in Morocco is one of the most spectacular mountain ranges of them all, an often snow-capped wall behind which the Sahara Desert is spread like a sandy carpet for thousands of miles. It's a dramatic piece of geography, then, and getting over it is no less of a drama. The two main passes through the Atlas are the Tizi n' Test

▼ **If Ait Benhaddou looks familiar that's probably because it's played a starring role in a number of Hollywood blockbusters.** *(Shutterstock)*

and the Tizi n' Tichka, and this route uses both, starting and finishing in the magical city of Marrakesh.

While Morocco might conjure up images of hot sun and palm trees, you do need to think about the weather with this one; in the winter the Tizi n' Test may be impassable due to snow and is subject to sudden changes in the weather at any time of the year – I was caught in a flash flood in July that completely washed away the main street in Asni once, many years ago.

Asni actually makes a relaxing first stop after leaving the hustle and bustle of Marrakesh and is a good jumping-off point for climbing Mount Toubkal, the highest mountain in North Africa at 4,167m (13,671ft) and a doable hike if you're reasonably fit – though you will need to put aside some days for this.

Toubkal is classified as moderately difficult, and the same could apply to the Tizi n' Test, for like the mountain it's not to be taken lightly: the surface can be poor, the road narrow, while it's a staircase of tight bends in places with not much beyond the edge except a long drop. But all this is well worth it because of the splendid views, especially at the top where – if conditions allow – you can see the sinuous road unwinding down the pass, the Souss valley and the High Atlas on either side. Places to visit along the way include the Tinmel Mosque, built in 1156 in a rosy-pink stone, which is one of only two mosques in Morocco open to non-Muslims.

At the end of the Tizi n' Test road lies the laid-back Berber market town of Taroudant, a good place to spend the night. From Taroudant it's an easy drive to Ouarzazate, known as a gateway to the Sahara Desert, with its huge Taourirt Kasbah. You should also visit Ait Benhaddou, which is about 19 miles (30km) away; a red mud-brick kasr (Berber fort) that's spectacular enough to have earned starring roles in *The Mummy*, *Jesus of Nazareth*, *Gladiator* and more recently *Game of Thrones*. You may well get a feeling of déjà vu.

From Ouarzazate the Tizi n' Tichka road will take you back to Marrakesh; 'Tichka' means 'difficult', though it's not quite the 'test' of the Test. But run together, these two passes make this loop a proper Moroccan adventure.

PLANNING NOTES

Start and finish: Marrakesh.
Distance: 460 miles (740km).
Time needed: Three or four days for the loop, plus at least two days in Marrakesh.
When to go: The Tizi n' Test can be impassable at times in the winter and snow can also fall on the Tizi n' Tichka. On the other hand, it's very hot in the summer, so spring and autumn might be best.
Vehicle: Unless you're trying this in the winter or you want to really explore the desert then a 2wd hire car

(available in Marrakesh) will be fine. Also, it's not so difficult to take your own car into the country by ferry from Spain…. Just an idea.
Beware of: The Tizi n' Test can be a little hairy and it requires concentration.
Detours, extensions and variations: Once you're south of the High Atlas there's a whole world of road trip adventure awaiting you, including trips out to the Dadès Gorge, or Zagora, with its tantalising sign: 'Timbuctu, 52 days by camel'.

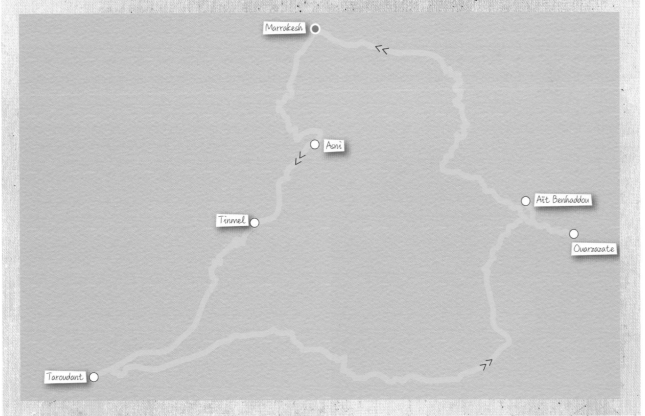

▲ **There are few countries that beat Tanzania when it comes to wildlife viewing.** *(Bresmedia)*

Rush hour in Dar es Salaam is big on hour, short on rush. You can easily find yourself waiting 20 minutes at a junction before a traffic cop waves your queue on. As you idle a carnival of vendors passes by, knocking on the windows, selling *everything*: sweets, peanuts, drinks, cakes, footballs, toolkits, car jacks, fish, mirrors, buckets, kites…

Maybe it's the traffic in the cities that prompts some guidebooks to say Tanzania is not a fly-drive destination? I can think of no other reason, as this was one of our best

▼ **It might look cute, but this little Toyota Rav 4 was tough enough for Tanzania.** *(Bresmedia)*

African road trips – which means it was one of our best road trips full stop.

It can be difficult to find a hire car, though, especially for a reasonable price, but after a little digging we discovered Roadtrip Tanzania, which offers old but very tough little Toyota Rav 4s which are more than up to the job, and bigger 4x4s too. You probably need a 4x4 of some sort, as while the roads are mostly in pretty good nick, as always in Africa expect gravel and rough stuff when you go off the beaten track, as you will have to in the game parks and to get to lodges and campsites.

That said, the route into the Serengeti is especially rough and probably best avoided unless you have a very well beefed-up vehicle. We paid for an extra safari as an add-on, which was expensive but worth it – high prices are a downside of Tanzania, along with overzealous police and border guards.

Our road trip route was Arusha to Tarangire (great for close encounters with elephants and walking safaris – 'we are now surrounded by the four most dangerous animals in Africa', whispered the guide). This is also close to Lake Manyara and the natural wonder that is the Ngorongoro Crater, so it is a great area for wildlife and also for Maasai culture.

From Tarangire we doubled back through Arusha and drove on to Moshi, which sits in the shadow of Mount

Kilimanjaro and is a base for hikes to the summit – I say in the shadow, but the shade is mostly from cloud, which means you rarely see the mountain. But we did just catch a glimpse of it as we left Moshi, heading for the Usambara Mountains for stunning views, encounters with chameleons and excellent hiking – avoid the local sugar cane beer.

The beer was fine on the tropical beaches of the Indian Ocean coast near Pangani, though, and it's a great place to chill. It's tempting to drive down the coast road all the way to Dar es Salaam from here, but when we were there the track – around Pangani at least – was in a very poor condition after heavy rains. Take local advice on this. The loop around to Dar was a great drive anyway; except for arriving in the unrushed rush hour.

PLANNING NOTES

Start and finish: Arusha to Dar es Salaam.
Distance: 684 miles (1,100km).
Time needed: The trip featured was completed in ten days.
When to go: It can be expensive in Tanzania, so think about the shoulder seasons. We went in July, which was fine (it rains most in April and May in the north), but this trip would be good at any time.
Vehicle: While the roads connecting the main towns are pretty good on the whole, if you're going into a reserve or along the coast, then a 4x4 would be useful, if only for the ground clearance.

Beware of: Most of the driving is pretty sedate but the dala dalas – brightly painted sardine-packed minibuses – are in a constant grand prix, so watch out for them. Prices for lodges and safaris can be on the high side while you might tire of Tanzanian bureaucracy.

Detours, extensions and variations: Once in Dar then Zanzibar is just a ferry ride away.

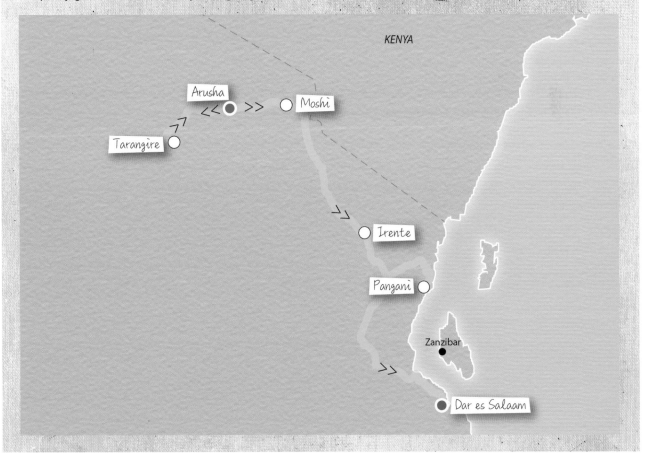

The white rhino was just five metres away. She was with her calf and was protective. I took a photograph and her ears flicked in alarm, then her horn scythed the air. The guide signalled that we should crouch down, pretend to be a bush. That did the trick.

Fair to say that Swaziland is big on thrills, then, but it's still quite a small country, and so linking it to a trip around KwaZulu-Natal (KZN) makes perfect sense. We drove out of Johannesburg, although this could also be done from Durban; but then you wouldn't get to pay a visit to the best toilet in the world. At the Alzu Petroport service station between Witbank and Belfast on the N4, the urinals face a half-glass wall that overlooks a field of antelope, ostrich, zebra and even rhinoceros. Beats reading pasted sports pages of *The Sun* as you go.

This trip took us to Waterval Boven (Emgwenya) first, and then there was probably the easiest of African border crossings to get us into Swaziland. We stopped in Phophonyane Falls (the lodge is a wonderful place with well-appointed beehive huts) and Hlane where we had the rhino encounter mentioned above – if rhinos are your thing then this is the place for you, I counted 13 around the main water hole one afternoon. There's much more to see and do in Swaziland, too, including other top-class game reserves and Ezulwini Valley, the traditional hub of tourism in the country.

Heading back into South Africa and further south is Hluhluwe-iMfolozi game park, a place of dramatically rolling hills, plentiful game and varied pronunciations. Then there's also the coast and the iSimangaliso Wetland Park. Nelson Mandela said of this: 'iSimangaliso must be the only place on

▲ **We had to crouch and keep very still when this white rhino got a bit agitated.** *(Bresmedia)*

the globe where the oldest land mammal [the rhinoceros] and the world's biggest terrestrial mammal [the elephant] share an ecosystem with the world's oldest fish [the coelacanth] and the world's biggest marine mammal [the whale].'

From Hluhluwe we drove south to stay on the beach near Durban at Salt Rock (try bunny chow, curry in a hollowed-out loaf of bread) before heading inland for a great drive to the Zulu War battlefields of Isandlwana and Rorke's Drift – read a book about it before you go and then get a different perspective from a Zulu guide when you're there.

From Isandlwana it's a long drive across the Free State back to Jo'burg, which looks a bit boring on the map, yet it's dotted with pleasant towns and breathtaking scenery. And if you do stay in the city then try to get to Soweto. It's an interesting place, in ways you might not expect.

▼ **The Zulu memorial at Rorke's Drift is especially poignant.** *(Bresmedia)*

PLANNING NOTES

Start and finish: Johannesburg.

Distance: 1,087 miles (1,750km).

Time needed: We did this in ten days, quite comfortably.

When to go: The coast of KZN is warm to hot the year round, while inland it's not much different until you gain height – though be prepared for sudden thunderstorms. Swaziland enjoys a good climate, though it can get a little cold on the higher ground in the winter. We went in May (autumn) and although there was a little rain, it was generally pretty good.

Vehicle: A two-wheel-drive hire car is fine though there are some unsealed roads to negotiate to get to lodges.

Beware of: There are always warnings to be especially careful when leaving Johannesburg's OR Tambo Airport in a hire car, as there have been carjackings in the past.

Detours, extensions and variations: It would not have been too much of a stretch to add a few days in the Drakensburg Mountains.

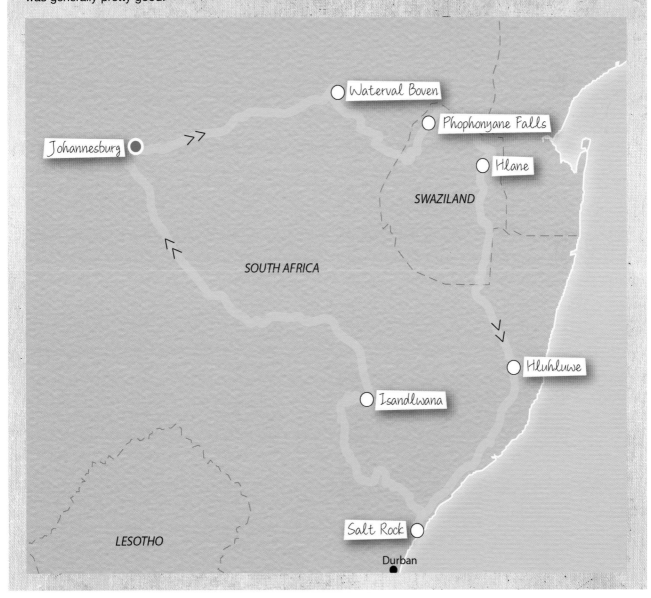

Johannesburg

Waterval Boven

Phophonyane Falls

Hlane

SWAZILAND

SOUTH AFRICA

Hluhluwe

Isandlwana

LESOTHO

Salt Rock

Durban

There are not so very many border crossings that also involve a switch from driving on one side of the road to the other, but Uganda/Rwanda is one of them. For this trip we crossed from Uganda into Rwanda, then back again, and each time we could not help but notice that both sides seemed to lack one rather important thing on entering: a sign to say 'here we drive on the right/left'. This is stranger still when you see how little used and twisty the run from the Gatuna crossing in the direction of Kigali is. Still, it's all part of the adventure.

And if you do this trip during the rainy season – we had hoped to catch the tail-end but it arrived late and was prolonged – there's plenty more adventure to be had, too.

▼ **Mountain gorilla with three-day-old baby in Bwindi Impenetrable Forest.** *(Bresmedia)*

▲ **Toyota Land Cruiser was the perfect vehicle for this trip.** *(Bresmedia)*

Indeed, in this one journey we got stuck in the mud twice; towed a minibus out of a quagmire; and took four attempts to make it up one hill (which itself was on the side of a long drop). And then there was the usual craziness you get at all times of the year to contend with: including everything from single beds to coffins (twice!) transversely loaded on motorbikes; being passed on blind bends and brows; and avoiding elephants. In short, it was amazing.

Because of the rains we were glad we'd hired a Toyota Land Cruiser – they are the workhorse of Africa for good reason, and it never let us down as we journeyed first from laid-back Entebbe on the shores of Lake Victoria to Lake Mburo National Park, before heading south to cross the border into Rwanda.

The roads in Rwanda are excellent, the driving standards less so, but seeing the modern skyscape of Kigali in the distance after miles of tea plantations and impossibly verdant scenery was memorable – it was like approaching Oz. The city's great, as is the drive to Lake Kivu; stay at Rubona, a tropical paradise with its own brewery. Could you ask for more?

On arriving back in Uganda we stayed at the jaw-dropping Lake Mutanda, which for us was the jump-off point for gorilla tracking in Bwindi Impenetrable National Park. This involved a drive along a very wet and hilly track, which was almost as exciting as getting within three metres of a grumpy silverback.

The next day was also a driving challenge. It just didn't seem possible that the single-lane rough track barely clinging to a mountain with no other vehicle on it could be a main road, but we trusted our planning and we were eventually rewarded with sightings of the famous tree lions in Ishasha, Queen Elizabeth National Park, where we also camped amidst a bunch of hippos. Lovely Fort Portal and

frantic Kampala followed, before we closed the loop in Entebbe.

The sheer adventure was the highlight of this trip, but it would be worth doing for the friendliness of the people we met in both countries alone.

PLANNING NOTES

Start and finish: Entebbe.

Distance: 1,118 miles (1,800km).

Time needed: This was a two-week trip.

When to go: Driving can be tricky in some places during the rainy seasons. Generally speaking, the big rains are from the middle of February to June and then there are also rains from September to December. The wettest times are April, May, October and November.

Vehicle: For getting to the very best places, 4wd is highly recommended, though town to town in Rwanda

and much of Uganda is certainly doable in a regular car. Yet even the black stuff will suddenly disappear from time to time.

Beware of: This is probably not the best option for a first trip in Africa; the driving on the highways – especially when it comes to buses – lacks imagination, while the traffic in the towns and cities is frantic (and fun!) and the rough stuff can be on the extreme side.

Detours, diversions and variations: In Uganda go north to Murchison Falls for more wildlife encounters; in Rwanda head east to Akagera National Park.

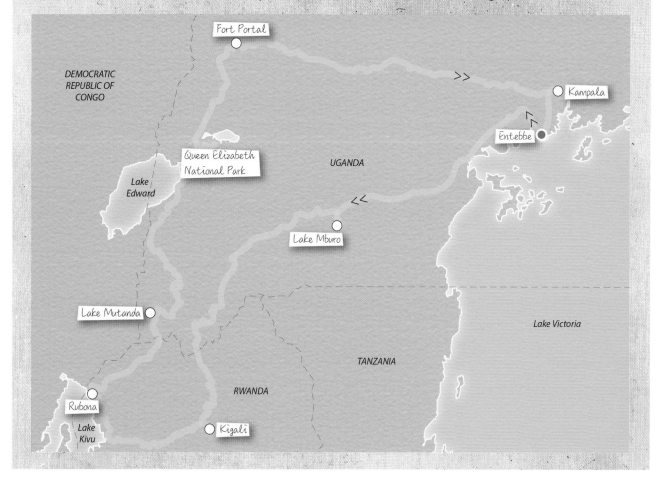

Chapter 6

ASIA

Asia is home to most of the people on the planet and yet also has some of its emptiest spaces. It is vast and has every road trip experience imaginable; whether it's tracing the dazzling Mediterranean coast of Turkey; forsaking the bullet train and hitting the expressways of Japan; exploring the deserts of Jordan and Oman; motorcycling in Thailand; or trying to make sense of Indian traffic. If you like your road trip with added spice, then Asia's for you.

◀ Camel crossing sand covered road in Dubai. *(Shutterstock)*

If the stunning scenery doesn't impress you then the awesome engineering of the expressways will – and let's not forget some of the best driving roads in the world, amazing food and a culture that is as foreign as it is fascinating. Welcome to Japan.

The earth shuddered, just for a moment or so. It's not unusual, in Japan. Some say this is because it lies on the Pacific Ring of Fire, the world's most active earthquake belt, where tectonic plates crunch and grind into each other like subterranean sumo wrestlers. But just perhaps there's another reason. Maybe the land's complaining? You wouldn't blame it, when you see just how many tunnels have been skewered through its mountainous crust to allow the passage of Japan's superb expressways.

And tunnels, uncountable in number and unfathomably long at times, are just a part of the engineering wonders that you will see on the expressways. For instance, you might be driving along a road only to suddenly realise it's been elevated, often very high, for many, many miles. This is best when it cuts through a city; it's a cross between speeding through an urban environment on a Hot Wheels track and being in a video game. But even this is trumped by the graceful suspension bridges,

▼ **The Irohazaka Winding Road near Nikko – it's clear to see how it got its name.** *(Shutterstock)*

or rather chains of bridges, which link the larger islands. Who said motorway driving is boring?

On the other hand, driving on the expressways is not cheap, so although necessary if you have a lot of the country to cover – as we did on our 1,491 mile (2,400km) road trip – it's sometimes much better to avoid the tolls and take the winding way. And the winding way does not come more winding than the Irohazaka Winding Road; home of the drifters.

But before we arrived there we had to pick up our car at Narita, which is one of the two international airports serving Tokyo. We chose one of the big rental companies, as this meant we could get an English-speaking satnav and the ETC card so we didn't need to stop at the manned toll booths on the expressways, and both proved invaluable (see The basics). From Narita it was an easy first stage to Nikko, which boasts some beautiful temples high in wooded hills and is also close to the Irohazaka Winding Road. In the night, kept awake by jet lag, the grumble of distant engines and the dragon sighs of dump valves could be heard. I should have taken those nocturnal noises as a clue that

▲ **This charming old bridge in Nikko is on the Romantic Road.** *(Bresmedia)*

the Winding Road is probably best visited in the hours of darkness, or at dawn, if it's a spirited drive, rather than just the glorious views, you're after.

As it was, it was a Monday morning in autumn when we drove along this serpentine stretch of road; but this is a popular season for holidaying in Japan – the leaves burn bright against azure skies – and while the road is a sort of loop, one-way and two-lane for most of its way, it was choked with traffic. It wasn't a waste, though, as the Kegon Falls just off the road are very impressive. Besides, as this is all part of the Romantic Road, we were going this way anyway.

The Romantic Road is a Japanese version of the themed drives in Germany, linking a number of beauty spots and places of interest. It's not especially well signposted along the way but it's easy enough to follow if you plan ahead and enter stages in the satnav (see Planning notes) rather than final destinations. Some parts of it offer a good driving experience, too, especially the Alpine-style roads after Lake Chuzenji – and people are super polite in Japan, even to the point of pulling over to let you through if you want to drive just a little bit quicker. I've seen that elsewhere, but not to this extent.

We stopped for the night at the chic resort of Karuizawa, then the next day took the expressways down to Nakatsugawa. The reason we chose this stop was so that we could hike a section of the old Edo Period Nakasendo post road between the quaint, preserved, little towns of Magome and Tsumago. It was a lovely walk, with free Japanese tea in a traditional tea house along the way. But the real highlight of Nakatsugawa was our local. One of our little rules for a road trip evening is to always go to local hostelries; rarely the hotel

bar. It's a way to see beneath the fingernails of a country. Izakayas are Japan's version of the local boozer, although they are as much about food as beer and sake. It takes a little time to figure out how they work, but that's all part of the fun.

One thing that's not so much fun in Japan is the parking in the cities, and so we planned ahead and tried to make sure everywhere we stayed had parking. At our next stop, Nara, this was actually a sort of vending machine for cars. I parked the car on an elevator platform, got out, and then it was

▼ **Nara's stunning Tōdai-ji is the world's largest wooden building.** *(Bresmedia)*

◀ The Great Buddha inside the Tödai-ji. *(Bresmedia)*

mechanically filed on a shelf above. A code is tapped in to bring it down when needed. This is quite common in Japan.

Nara is worth any amount of parking hassle, though. It's impossible to do justice to its staggering Tödai-ji, the world's largest wooden building, or the immense bronze Daibutsu (Great Buddha) within, in words or even pictures. Like the Pyramids of Giza or Victoria Falls, this is something that needs to be seen.

From Nara it was a spellbinding drive along an elevated expressway that seemed to float among the tower blocks of Osaka and Kobe. It went on for miles, and the best of it was the sweeping curve to the right when we hit the coast: so high that there were many layers of roadways beneath us, with the Osaka port and a toy ship dotted sea ahead. Truly stunning; as were the bridges that took us across to Awaji Island and then the large island of Shikoku beyond.

Shikoku is just a little off the beaten track; but verdant and bountiful, like driving through a salad. We stayed at a marvellous hotel called Momijigawa Onsen. The onsen in the name refers to the hot spring baths, which were a feature of a few of the hotels we stayed at. But this was one of the best of them, and certainly the most unpretentious. Using an onsen is a naked thing – men and women use different baths, with a slightly complicated etiquette which often includes no tattoos – apparently in Japan this is a sign that you're a gangster. In Momijigawa Onsen there was an outside hot pool overlooking the lake-like section of the dammed Naka River, with shrieking kites swooping metres overhead. Memorable.

As was breakfast. This place was very Japanese with little English spoken. Breakfast was a tray of dishes, half of which we could not recognise. It's an exciting way to start the day, and when a dish that seemed to contain a brain from a small animal and Lego blocks in WD40 ended up tasting like potatoes, stuffing and gravy, quite surprising too.

Shikoku is a surprising island, with some beautiful temples, lovely secluded beaches and some of the best driving we found in Japan. The route from Momijigawa Onsen to the Iya Valley, along 195, 193, 438 and then the well-known 439 is really something. It's mostly single track, winding its way through the Dosa Pass, with its rough-hewn tunnel, and then up the slopes of the 2,000m (6,561ft) Mount Tsurugi before reaching the Iya Valley. A tip here, coming from the east like this you arrive at East Iya first, rather than the crowded tourist trap that is West Iya. In East Iya there are two swaying vine

◀ Nara's wild deer are very friendly, while they also know how to cross the road safely. *(Bresmedia)*

BY THE WAY ...

Declutching at straws

On the narrow Route 439 in Shikoku, Japan, sits the tiny village of Nagoro. You might suppose they have a crow problem in these parts, for the place is stuffed with scarecrows, whole families of the things. Some are posed working in a small field, others seem to be waiting for a bus, there's even a house full of them. But this is nothing to do with scaring crows and these figures were actually made by a lady in the village, Ayano Tsukimi, as a way of memorialising past residents, which is sweet. But I guess they still scare off the birds.

▶ **Vine bridge in East Aya Valley – don't worry, you will not need to drive across this.** *(Bresmedia)*

bridges you can cross on foot, with quite big gaps between the slats so you can see the torrent below – so the adventure didn't end with the driving on this day of the journey.

Plunging down from the Iya Valley the drive is not so wild, but still spectacular, but nature's eclipsed when you take the expressway to cross back on to Japan's main island of Honshu. The Seto-Ohashi crossing is actually a series of double-deck suspension bridges making one continuous crossing – the longest two-tiered bridge in the world. The view of the islands far, far below and the ships scoring white lines in the Seto Inland Sea is simply staggering.

▼ **Tranquil garden in Himeji with the top of the castle just visible in the background.** *(Bresmedia)*

▲ **The Golden Temple – or Kinkaku-ji – in Kyoto.** *(Bresmedia)*

◄ **This traditional hotel room in Hakone was short on clutter yet very comfortable.** *(Bresmedia)*

Himeji Castle is a more classical view; Japan on a chocolate box, complete with actors dressed up as scary ninjas. After our stop there we drove to Uji, and travelled in to central Kyoto from there on a small train which gave us a taste of Japanese railways. There was actually a bit of a minor panic at the station as the train was late. We thought we'd be in for a long wait. But the drama was over a *two-minute delay*.

Kyoto's temples are spectacular, while the way Japanese tourists dress up as geishas to wander around is, well, curious. There are real geishas, too, as elegant as the towering pagoda. The golden Kinkaku-ji, which seems to float over its reflection in a large pond, was quite breathtaking, but after seeing so many temples already by then perhaps the real highlight of Kyoto was the Nishiki Market, with its mix of strange and familiar sights and smells, and a street food lunch of fish on a stick.

The longest drive of the entire trip came next; from Uji to Hakone, near Mount Fuji. We had been lucky with the weather until now, but this day the many tunnels along the expressway proved a respite from the driving rain. Suzuka National Park, which the expressway passed through, was a

◄ **The Hakone Turnpike is Japan's answer to the Nürburgring – get there early in the morning and you'll have the road to yourself.** *(Bresmedia)*

sight though; the mist boiling off the tree-clad hills like smoke from forest fires.

We stayed in a traditional Japanese room in Hakone, with futons on the tatami floor and boots and shoes checked in at reception, but it was a newer tradition that brought us here. The Hakone Turnpike has been called Japan's Nürburgring. It's maybe even better than that, and certainly cheaper. This is where the Japanese motoring mags test cars. It's two-way traffic, with one direction mostly uphill and the other downhill, with a lovely pair of quite long switchback turns along the way. Because it's a toll road it's usually quiet too – there are no Irohazaka-style traffic jams here. The downhill direction is super quick, with escape roads in case your brakes run out. At the bottom of the descent we burst through the mist and into bright sunlight, a bullet train slicing the view of the sparkling Sagami Bay ahead of us. It was an enjoyable moment; encapsulating our Japanese road trip.

That might have been the ideal place to conclude this account; but Japan keeps giving, and driving right through the centre of Tokyo on the expressway, level with the middle floors of tall buildings, was an incredible experience. My only regret was that I didn't get the chance to do the same at night.

PLANNING NOTES

Start and finish: Narita Airport, Tokyo.

Distance: 1,491 miles (2,400km).

Time needed: We took 12 days, including a couple in Tokyo at the end, which made this trip quite a relaxed one, while we still covered a lot of ground.

When to go: Autumn can be spectacular, as is spring in the cherry blossom season, but this means it can be very busy in places. Winter will mean snow and some closed roads in the mountains. June and July can be rainy, while the high season is April to May and August.

Vehicle: If hiring a car, make sure you have an English-speaking satnav, while an ETC card for paying tolls automatically is also recommended if you're planning to use the expressways.

Beware of: The big expense is the tolls and if you want to cover a lot of ground you need to factor this in. Also, while many petrol stations are manned, self-service stations are fully automated and can be a challenge if there are no English instructions. There's usually someone around to help, though.

Detours, extensions and variations: It would have been nice to cross from Shikoku across the Shimanami Kaido to visit Hiroshima and then head to Himeji from there.

Further info: For more on the Romantic Road go to: www.japan-guide.com and search 'romantic road'.

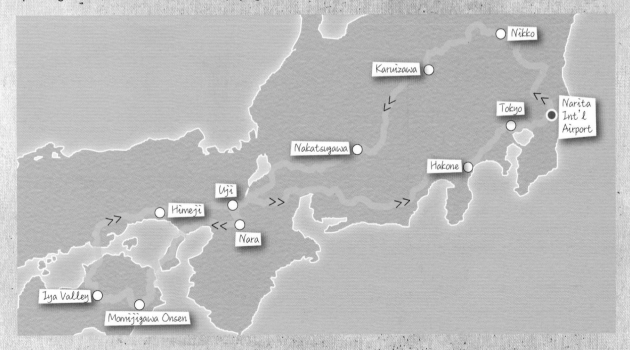

▲ Pamukkale, which means 'cotton castle' in Turkish, is an extraordinary place. *(Shutterstock)*

Something was bound to go wrong with it at some point. It was an old car, and a cheap car, and it had already been driven across Europe before we had even got to Turkey. We were just glad that it was a relatively small problem – the exhaust had fallen off. I managed to tie it up with a bit of string and then we went looking for the nearest town and its 'auto alley', the cluster of workshops that seem to be on the edge of every settlement in Turkey. It took 45 minutes to make and weld a bracket, while they marvelled at the steering wheel being in the wrong place, and we drank little glasses of their tea. It cost £2.

That was Turkey back then, but it's not changed so much since. It's still a friendly country, and it still offers up great opportunities for road trip adventure. We drove a loop that starts from Istanbul and heads down the Gallipoli Peninsula to Eceabat. To get to Asia properly you need to cross the Dardanelles on the ferry to Çanakkale, then you can stop off to visit the site of Troy. There's not much remaining of Troy itself, but there's plenty of Pergamon left, including the ancient theatre built into the hillside. This is pretty impressive, as is Ephesus – I was also really taken by the crumbling ancient aqueduct in the centre of the nearby town of Selçuk, with its storks nesting on the old supporting pillars.

Hierapolis is an intriguing ancient site, too, but you will always remember it as Pamukkale, which means 'cotton castle' in Turkish; referring to the glistening white limestone terraces that have been formed by calcium deposits. It's a surreal place.

After a great drive during a thunderstorm we spent a few days at the lovely little town of Kaş, before

◄ Our Polo parked in front of pixie chimneys in Göreme. *(Bresmedia)*

heading further along the Mediterranean coast. At one point we were stuck in a queue for hours, not moving an inch. We never discovered why; and no one else seemed to care, breaking out picnics and footballs, offering us biscuits. Turkey can be like that.

A few days later, crossing the Taurus Mountains to head inland again, we came across the most colourful accident ever. A lorry had hit the bank and turned on to its side, spilling its cargo of oranges that rolled down the hillside. We actually saw the aftermath of quite a few accidents. Turkey can be like that, too.

An arrow-straight drive along the Anatolian Plain then took us to Göreme in Cappadocia, where you can stay the night in a cave hotel amidst an enchanting landscape of 'fairy chimney' rock formations. Magical. We drove back to Istanbul via Ankara, but whichever way you go, make sure you have time to explore Istanbul properly; it's a wonderful city.

PLANNING NOTES

Start and finish: Istanbul.
Distance: 1,647 miles (2,650km).
Time needed: Three weeks to do this justice.
When to go: Spring and autumn are the best times for this trip.
Vehicle: We did this in an old VW Polo so pretty much anything will do and picking up a hire car at Istanbul Airport works well.

Beware of: Driving standards can be pretty dire in Turkey and road accidents are common. It's particularly dangerous in the hour before the fast-breaking meal during Ramadan, they say.
Detours, extensions and variations: Turkey is a surprisingly big country and extending the loop to the east to take in Mount Nemrut (with its massive stone heads) and other sites is well worth thinking about.

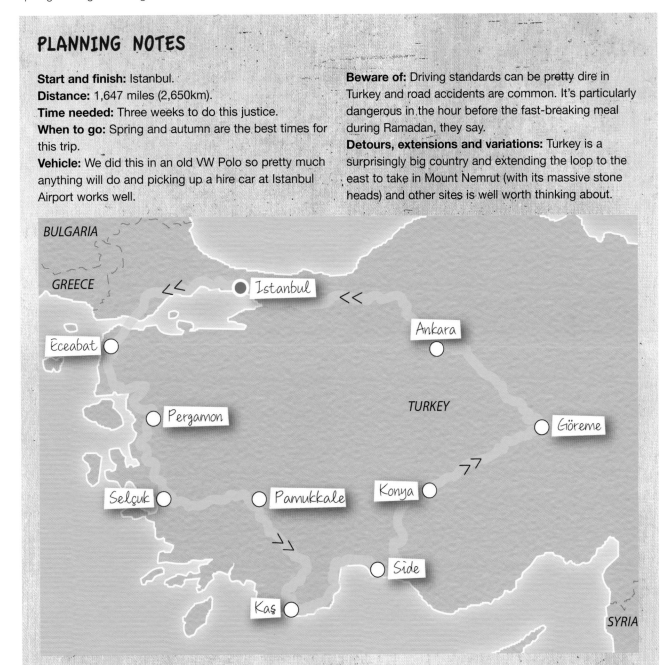

▲ **Might he have found room for just a little bit more stuff on this truck? There's always plenty to ponder on an Indian road trip.** *(Salvador Aznar / Shutterstock)*

Is it a road trip if you're not driving yourself? I'm not entirely sure, but everyone said it was just not feasible to self-drive in India. I wish I hadn't listened. But then over 1,240 miles (2,000km) sitting in the back of a tin can that called itself a Maruti-Suzuki Omni and had no seat padding nor air conditioning in the June heat does tend to make you review your decisions. So, if I did it again, I'd drive myself. Would I do it again? You bet!

The reason we took a car (well a mini-mini-micro-bus) and driver for our trip around Rajasthan was because it was dirt cheap. Our driver, Chani, liked a whisky or two yet that didn't seem to affect his skill – he missed a sacred cow with a deft piece of evasive driving once. But then that's the thing with India, there are lots of things to miss; often coming the wrong way up a divided road! We also saw a lot of overturned trucks, a few overturned buses, and a motorbike with five people on it – this is only worth mentioning as it wasn't four, there were plenty with four.

Our route was Delhi (the traffic has to be seen to be believed); before our first stop in Rajasthan at Jhunjhunu (nice havelis; grand houses); then dusty Bikaner (the impressive Junagarh Fort); Jaisalmer (an interesting fort town, but the best was riding camels in the Thar Desert then sleeping under the stars); Jodhpur (the Blue City; it really is, with the mighty Mehrangarh Fort towering over it); then a stop at the marble Jain temple at Ranakpur, a stunning

◀ **Rajasthan is not short of stunning architecture to admire – this is the Lake Palace in Udaipur.** *(Shutterstock)*

BY THE WAY ...

Cosmic cycle

One evening in 1991 local villager Om Banna crashed his 350cc Enfield Bullet motorcycle into a tree on a stretch of road 5 miles (8km) south of Rohat, near. Chotila village, on the Pali and Udaipur road from Jodhpur, in Rajasthan, India. Poor Om was killed, and the bike was taken back to the local police station; only to return to the scene of the accident – seemingly by itself! The police took it back, chained it up, and emptied the tank of petrol. Yet again it returned to the crash site, and it kept doing so. Naturally, this was grounds for the motorbike to be deified and a temple to be set up close to the tree that had killed Om. It's called Om Banna Temple and features the magic Enfield and, perhaps ironically given its history, it's where travellers will pray for a safe journey.

place, before Udaipur (the vast City Palace and Lake Palace, of James Bond *Octopussy* fame); holy Pushkar; Jaipur (the Amber Palace was impressive but even more memorable was taking in a Bollywood film at the Raj Mindir cinema); then Agra for the Taj Mahal (which needs no introduction, but try to get there early and don't bother with a guide).

We probably went at the wrong time as it was very, very hot, but the monsoon brought relief in the afternoons, and also a hold-up one day when the road flooded. It was great fun to watch the trucks and Mahindra Jeeps, and then the buses, and then the Hindustan Ambassadors and the donkey carts, wade through the deluge, as the level slowly diminished. But we had to wait until last, as our engine was under the floor, and the floor was low. Yes, when I go to India again, I'll hire a car: a nice tall one with springy, soft seats and air conditioning.

PLANNING NOTES

Start and finish: Delhi.
Distance: 1,367 miles (2,200km).
Time needed: We did this in 12 days, which seemed about right.
When to go: We went in late June and into July, which was probably a mistake. It was insanely hot in Delhi, while the rains came on big time. December to February is high season but the shoulders make sense (September to November and February to March).
Vehicle: Hire cars are available in Delhi but if you do opt for a car and driver instead then avoid an Ambassador; they may look stately but they are also very slow.
Beware of: It's hard to find parking spaces and road rules are, err, fluid. If you're happy to accept that as part of the adventure, then hire a car. If not, hire a car and driver. The latter course does have its advantages. Also, watch out for scams of all sorts, especially in big cities and tourist hot spots. Common sense will see you right.
Detours, extensions and variations: If you're pushed for time, then the Golden Triangle – Delhi, Jaipur, Agra then back to Delhi – might suit you better.

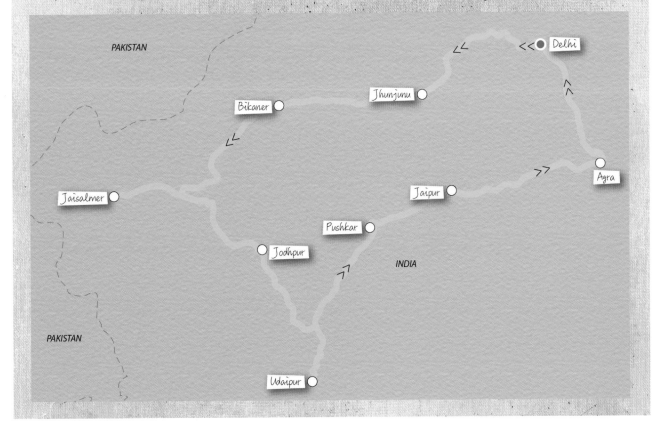

The Mae Hong Son loop is a popular journey for motorbikes or scooters that is often offered as a four-day tour. As the name suggests, the route explores the mountainous and lushly-forested Mae Hong Son Province and over its 400 miles (650km), riders – or indeed drivers – can expect awesome views, interesting towns and villages in which to overnight, and quite distinctive regional cuisine. In fact, this remote province in the north-west corner of Thailand has a character all of its own, to the extent that some even say it can seem like a completely different country.

The loop starts and ends at Chiang Mai, the cultural capital of the north of Thailand, with its lively nightlife, many temples and historic Old City, but it really starts to get interesting when you join Route 1095, with its 1,864 bends, 21 miles (35km) north of the city. To begin with the 1095 climbs slowly but pretty dramatically – the most challenging driving or riding on the loop – towards the delightfully situated town of Pai (stop off at Pai Canyon on the way). You

▼ **The Mae Hong Son loop is often offered as a tour, with motorcycle hire included, in Chiang Mai.**

(Matyas Rehak / Shutterstock)

▶ **The roads aren't too bad on the loop; but you can never be sure what you might meet around the next corner.** *(Shutterstock)*

then head on to Sop Pong, which while it offers little in the way of sights itself is a great base from which to explore the Pamg Mapha district's many cave systems. There are over 200 caves, but Tham Lot, 5 miles (8km) north of Sop Pong, is one of the most doable and also one of the largest in Thailand, at 1,600m (5,250ft) in length. Guides and lanterns are available, and mandatory. You can also walk to one of the hill tribe villages from Sop Pong.

From Sop Pong it's on to Mae Hong Son itself, which with its location near the border with Myanmar has a distinctly Burmese feel and boasts some impressive temples, while it is a great place from which to set off on treks into the mountainous forests. Long-tail boat trips on the Mae Nam Pai river are also very popular with backpackers and road trippers alike.

Some 43 miles (70km) south of Mae Hong Son is the quiet hillside town of Khun Yuam, from where you take Route 108 to Mae Sariang (a small town with a real off-the-beaten-track feel to it) and then loop back to Chiang Mai.

PLANNING NOTES

Start and finish: Chiang Mai.

Distance: 404 miles (650km).

Time needed: This is often advertised as a four-day motorcycle tour.

When to go: The cool season, November to January, is the best time as it's dry and not too hot. The monsoon rains are between July and September, so this is probably not a great time for riding a bike.

Vehicle: The roads are mostly paved, and if a moped's not for you then you can always hire a car in Chiang Mai.

Beware of: A report in 2014 found that Thailand's roads are the second most dangerous in the world, so you do need to be careful. If you're hiring a motorbike, make sure you thoroughly check it over and that you're given a decent helmet.

Detours, extensions and variations: On the last leg of the loop you can turn off to Doi Inthanon National Park, which is home to the mountain of the same name – Thailand's highest at 2,565m (8,415ft). Climb to the summit and explore the jungle hiking trails. You can also head directly here from Khun Yuam, and then shorten the loop back to Chiang Mai.

MYANMAR

Sop Pong ○

Pai ○

Mae Hong Son ○

Khun Yuam ○

Chiang Mai ●

Mae Sariang ○

THAILAND

▲ Omani roads are in good condition and fuel is cheap – a great place for a road trip then. *(Shutterstock)*

▼ Nizwa Fort is a highlight of our Omani loop. *(Shutterstock)*

What sets Oman apart from some of its neighbours is that it's not rushed headlong into sky-high development and the country retains much of its charm because of this. But it also has excellent roads, cheap fuel, no shortage of parking, and a rugged beauty that's hard to equal. Perfect road trip country, then.

Muscat, the sea-hugging ribbon of a capital, is easy to get to – either flying in or driving down from Dubai as many do – and is a fascinating city, especially the Muttrah Souk, a great place to haggle. Our loop starts from here and then traces the coast to the town of Sur – via a swim at the sinkhole at Hawiyat Najm Park. Picturesque Sur once played a pivotal role in Oman's trade with East Africa and it's now home to the last remaining shipyard for building wooden dhows – never using plans but just by eye – which is well worth a visit. By the way, some say the legendary sailor Sinbad once called Sur his home. From Sur you can take a detour of around 30 miles (50km) along the dramatic coastal road to the Ras Al Jinz Turtle Reserve (turtles can be seen all year round but September to October is the best time).

After the delights of the Gulf of Oman it's time to head inland and the desert proper, and also places like Wadi Bani Khalid. Reached via a graded dirt track this long wadi is a

true, lush oasis – walk for a while along it to find the best swimming spots. Less than an hour from Wadi Bani Khalid along Highway 23 is Bidyah, a good place for the many desert experiences that are available in Oman, such as glamping in the dunes.

Heading north, it's a great day's drive to Nizwa, the capital of Oman in the 6th and 7th centuries, and a town that is dominated by the huge circular tower of its very impressive fort, which also offers great views of the blue- and gold-domed mosque – the souk is also pretty cool. From Nizwa you can visit Bahla Fort, which is not only the oldest castle in Oman but also the largest. The town has a reputation for strange happenings – flying mosques and magic trees for a start – but is also, more prosaically, famed for its pottery.

Jebel Shams is the last stop before returning to Muscat via Highway 15. It's perfect hiking territory, with plenty of interesting villages to visit on the way there, and also once you're up in the mountains.

PLANNING NOTES

Start and finish: Muscat.
Distance: 560 miles (900km).
Time needed: A week to ten days.
When to go: It goes without saying that it gets hot in the summer, up to 48°C (118°F) in fact. We visited in January and the weather was pretty close to perfect.
Vehicle: While a 4wd will open up a world of exciting opportunities, the trip described here is doable in a regular hire car. Driving is very easy in Oman.
Beware of: You may have a problem getting a drink,

and while most of the hotels do sell alcohol, it's expensive. Also, if you really like a beer after a day's driving through the desert then don't visit during Ramadan.
Detours, extensions and variations: Not so far from Muscat and also a possible detour at the end of the trip is the Rustaq Loop, which runs for 155 miles (250km) from Barka on Highways 13 and 11 and takes in three of Oman's finest castles, at Nakhal, Rustaq and Al Hazm, as well as some splendid mountain scenery.

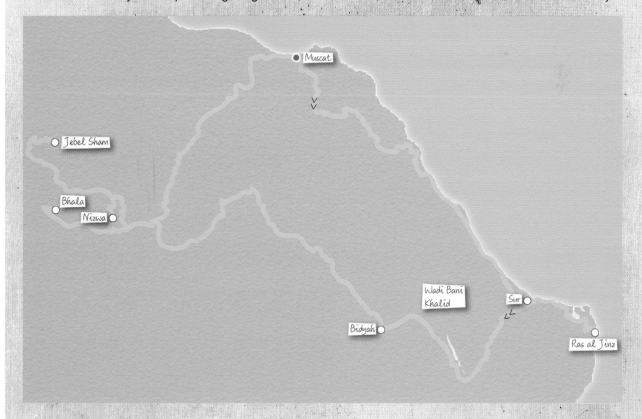

The first sight of Petra is dramatic. You feel a bit like Indiana Jones as you wind your way down the narrow serpentine fissure in the rock – the Siq – to the Treasury; a breathtaking tomb carved out of sandstone. Go early enough in the morning and it's easy to imagine what Jean Louis Burckhardt was feeling when he 'discovered' this place in 1812.

Petra alone makes Jordan worth a visit. Throw in a Rome's-worth of other historical sites and the unbeatable spectacle of Wadi Rum and it's simply a must-*see*. Then add floating in the Dead Sea like a fly on a pint of ale and some cracking driving roads and it's also a must-*do*.

If you're heading south from Amman then there are three roads: the King's Highway, which is the focus of this trip; the Dead Sea Highway; and the Desert Highway, which means a loop is possible. The latter of these is the quickest way back to your starting point, but the Dead Sea Highway, which has the distinction of being the lowest drive in the world (430m, or 1,410ft, below sea level at one point), has more to offer in terms of things to see and do.

Amman itself is worth a couple of days of your time. It's a friendly and vibrant place with some cool sites, including a well-preserved Roman theatre and the winding lanes, atmospheric souks and coffee shops that make Middle Eastern cities such a joy – and don't miss the excellent Royal Automobile Museum.

With the car museum having put you in the mood, it's time to hit the King's Highway, which, although it's known for its sights, is actually a pretty good driving road in places. The route runs down the middle of Jordan's central highlands, from Madaba (Byzantine mosaics), then crossing the 'Grand Canyon of Jordan' at Wadi Mujib before arriving at the site of the impressive 12th-century Crusader castle at Kerak. Dana, a great base for hiking, is also worth a stop or stay.

And then there's Petra, which is simply unmissable, with enough to see and do for two days. From there it's on to

▼ **Jordan's King's Highway as it twists through Wadi Mujib.**
(Shutterstock)

▶ **Al Khazneh, also known as the Treasury, in the ancient city of Petra.** *(Shutterstock)*

my favourite place in Jordan, Wadi Rum, made famous by T. E. Lawrence (of Arabia), one of the most beautiful desert landscapes on earth, and a great place to sleep out under a canopy of a billion-billion stars. If you can't nod off, try counting them.

Sometimes beach sand is welcome after desert sand, and Aqaba on the Red Sea offers that. There's also scuba diving, if that's your thing, but don't save that for the Dead Sea on the way back as the water's dense with salt and it's more about floating than swimming. The experience is quite surreal, though, as the water suspends you; the first time I tried it I read a copy of *Autosport* in the sea as if I was sat in an armchair.

PLANNING NOTES

Start and finish: Amman.
Distance: 478 miles (770km).
Time needed: The journey's not long, so it depends on how much you want to see and do, but you would not get bored spending a week on this.
When to go: The very best time for this is spring. It can get extremely hot in the summer in the desert, while on the higher ground surprisingly cold in the winter.
Vehicle: While a 4x4 would be perfect, especially for reaching the sites off the main road, an ordinary hire car will do the job.
Beware of: Despite it being so close to well-known trouble spots Jordanians are proud of how safe their country is. The driving is pure Middle East, though, and while it's easy enough outside of towns you might want to avoid taking a car into the chaos of Amman.
Detours, extensions and variations: A great drive out of Amman is the Desert Castle loop, which is a string of early-Islamic and older ruins. My favourite is Qasr al-Azraq, where T. E. Lawrence had his winter headquarters in the winter of 1917–18.

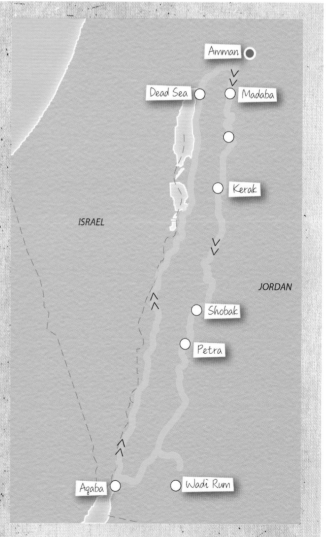

Chapter 7
LATIN AMERICA

From the world's driest desert to the towering Andean peaks, the glaciers of Patagonia to the verdant jungles of Costa Rica, Latin America offers every style of road trip you can imagine. Whether you enjoy threading your car or bike through teeming cities throbbing with life, exploring ghost towns in Chile, or taking the laid-back and lazy way from Rio to São Paulo, then South America, Central America, Mexico and Cuba will offer a road trip that's right for you.

◀ Campervan on the road from Los Glaciares National Park in Argentina. *(reisegraf.ch / Shutterstock)*

Cuba is an excellent road trip location with little in the way of traffic and lots in the way of sights – and if you ever tire of the wonderful old American cars then there's always the sublime beaches.

Driving out of Trinidad, into the enchanting Valle de los Ingenios. On one side of the road there's a leather-faced *guarijo* in a cowboy hat, a cigar clamped between his teeth and a machete dangling from his belt. Look the other way and the low morning sun lights up the flowing blue fender of an oncoming 1954 Chevrolet, transforming it into a dazzling aquamarine. I might have stopped to take a picture. But that's the problem with Cuba, if you halted for every photo opportunity it would take you a day to cover nine miles.

We took nine days to cover 900 miles (1,450km), and yes, there were a few stops for photographs. But the camera was busy even before we set off, in Havana. People often say they want to go to Cuba before it's too late. And it's still not too late, as even in the capital Cuba is still Cuba. There are still the queues at food shops, and empty shelves within, and there is still the sometimes baffling and often maddening bureaucracy, but there is also so much that you will not find anywhere else in the world: including, of course, the many, many old American cars.

The 'Yank Tanks' are leftovers from before the revolution. Cuba turned communist at the end of the 1950s and for decades was completely cut off from much of the world. This meant that things had to last, and Cubans became ingenious mechanics as they kept their Chevrolets, Dodges, Fords, Buicks and Plymouths alive. Often, but not always, this has involved a heart transplant and many of these cars now pack Lada or Moskvitch engines (Russian cars being the only imports for many years), but they are still quite a sight. Not a rare sight, either, and although there are modern cars now, as well as those from the old Eastern Bloc, a rough estimate would be that about 30% of all cars and trucks are pre-1959 and originated in the USA – this flies in the face of what's said on the internet, but then we were there and we were counting. Mind you, once you get out into the country they're not all quite as gleaming as the tourist-trip examples in Havana.

▼ **A bustling street in Cuba's capital, Havana.** *(Bresmedia)*

▲ Colour and classic cars: the essence of Cuba on a Trinidad back street. *(Bresmedia)*

▲▼ Some of the old American cars are in pretty good nick. *(Bresmedia)*

might be, as there's no satnav coverage and signposting is patchy at best. But by using a good old map and the helpful maps.me app we had downloaded before flying to Cuba we only lost our way once or twice.

One place where it is difficult to get lost – although not impossible on the outskirts of Havana – is on the autopistas (motorways), which we used to get to our first stop at Viñales, after local advice not to take our original route across the top of the island as part of this is in very poor condition.

The autopistas tend to be dual carriageways with three lanes each side, which seem even wider due to the lack of traffic. You will often find yourself alone as you drive these highways, which is actually quite useful as it gives you time to avoid the potholes; as much a fact of life on the motorways as they are on country roads and city streets. There was one section of autopista later in the trip that was particularly interesting where we were funnelled into a vague contraflow – though it was more of a hint than a clear sign – so we had the pleasure of speeding towards oncoming traffic while dodging rough patches of asphalt knowing that that oncoming traffic was doing exactly the same. As I said; 'interesting'.

Luckily, the traffic was light, and this is because few Cubans own cars and many get around by hitching. There are even officials who will stop cars which are then legally obliged to give lifts. I was aware of this so stopped near the autopista turn-off to Viñales when a man with a badge flagged us down to give another guy a lift. But it was soon clear our passenger was a tout looking for tourist business (a jintero as they're called). This was a one-off, though, and because we'd booked ahead – often necessary if you want to stay in casa particulares,

▲ **Take a peak under the bonnet of many of the Cuban classics and you're more likely to find a Russian four-pot than an American V8.** *(Bresmedia)*

Even though we were not in a fine old 1950s classic we drove out of Havana in some style, along the Malecón, the wide esplanade where the sea can crash dramatically over the wall to give passing automobiles a briny car wash. Navigating the length of the Malecón is simple enough, but finding your way around the rest of Cuba is not as easy as it

▼ **The distinctive scenery around Viñales with a tobacco drying shed to the left of the small farm, or finka.** *(Bresmedia)*

▼ **Pillbox in paradise: it's difficult to escape reminders of the past in the Bay of Pigs.** *(Bresmedia)*

BY THE WAY ...

Sign of the times

In Cuba there was many a time when we would have loved to see a simple roadside sign to tell us we were heading the right way or not, but these are rare. Yet while there are not many signs that point you in the direction you want to go, there are plenty of signs that remind you where the country has been. This one is typical, on the autopista (that's the motorway, as you can tell by the horse and rider!) in Sancti Spiritus province. It shows Camilo Cienfuegos and, of course, Che Guevara, and translates as 'the stage of struggle and victories', referring to the local exploits of these two Cuban heroes during the revolution in the 1950s. Propaganda signs like these are wonderful, if only because they remind you that you're in Cuba, and that Cuba is still a very different place.

which are family homes/guesthouses and are by far the best accommodation option in Cuba – we didn't really need somewhere else to stay anyway.

Jinteros aside, Viñales is a delight; set among distinctive flat-topped 'magotes' (limestone monoliths) and surrounded by outlandishly verdant fields speckled with little farms, or fincas, many of which grow tobacco for Cuba's most famous product, the Havana cigar. It's good for hiking too, or if that's too much effort there are horses you can hire. There are lots of horses in Cuba, many of them on the road.

There are even horses on the motorway, in fact, as we discovered on the long drive to Playa Larga, where you can now actually buy a Coke – nothing in itself, perhaps, until you realise that this particular stretch of sand was one of the landing sites for the ill-fated US-backed Bay of Pigs invasion. Couldn't help thinking they got there in the end – maybe the saying should go 'commerce is war by other means'?

Further around the bay at Playa Giron there's a museum to the Bay of Pigs debacle, or great victory – tick where appropriate – which is interesting, while there are many propaganda posters along the road. If you didn't know there had been a fight here in 1961 on arrival, you certainly would by the time you left.

History is gentler in Cienfuegos. This city has a different feel to others in Cuba, but it's the way the light plays along the pastel palette of the colonnade in the main street that makes it memorable. Well, that and the faded grandeur of Club Cienfuegos, once a yacht club but now a government-run bar and restaurant, where the food is a trip back to the 1970s.

It's more 1770s in nearby Trinidad, said to be the most perfectly preserved city in Latin America. Visiting its Plaza Mayor is like walking into a Mexico-set western movie; the genre confused when a 1956 Oldsmobile 88 thrums across the cobbles. Getting out of Trinidad was a little dramatic, too. It was a Saturday morning and traffic wasn't so bad, but every turn we took led to a closed street and a bored-looking cop who did little to point us in the right direction. Turns out there was some sort of festival going on, lots of little girls in best dresses, majorettes, and – as always –

▼ **Even in Cuba, Trinidad seems like it's from another time.**
(Bresmedia)

▲ **This is about as busy as the autopistas get.** *(Bresmedia)*

banners depicting Che Guevara, Fidel Castro and Camilo Cienfuegos. For a little while we somehow became part of the procession, but no one seemed to mind.

Driving out of, or through, Cuban towns and cities is seldom such a drama, even at rush hour. That's not to say it is like driving in towns in Europe or North America; it's far from that. It's more calmly chaotic, in a way; cars, bikes, bicycle taxis, horse-drawn carts and pedestrians all drifting along and across the road, never really quickly. It's like gas,

▼ **The abandoned Gran Hotel in San Miguel de los Banos is an atmospheric place to explore – but watch out for bees and falling masonry.** *(Bresmedia)*

Cuban traffic, and as is the case in many other countries you just need to go with the flow.

Out on the open road things speed up a bit, well the taxis do at least, otherwise there are a lot of very slow things to overtake, which means you need to have your wits about you. It's the one-horsepower stuff that's the real problem, and that takes patience – particularly as many roads seem to feature blind brows that are not always marked with warning signs. Also, not all cars have indicators, while some drivers seem to think they're just a pulsating styling device to be left on at all times, whichever way the car is turning. But all that aside, driving in Cuba is a delight.

The best of this driving was the sinuous road up to Viñales from the autopista; or tracing the coast round the Bay of Pigs, always close to the sparkling sea so it's nothing to park up and take a quick dip; then the drive from Cienfuegos to Trinidad, which wasn't long but encompassed lush tropical scenery and a spectacular stretch along the coast that included long bridges spanning estuaries – in parts it reminded me of Highway 1 in California, but nowhere near as busy. Also, the drive from Trinidad to Sancti Spiritus was both scenic and twisting.

As we headed up to Varradero to finish our trip with a day or two on the beach, we were forced off our chosen route through Colon when we discovered that the road we were *actually* driving on was *actually* closed. We never found out why, but our new route took us through some collective farms and interesting small country towns and was probably better anyway.

The drive from Varadero back to Havana was an unexpected delight, too, along the Via Blanca, with fine views out to sea, 'wish we'd stayed in' Matanza, and a surreal and stinking gas plant, right on the edge of the iridescent Florida Straits, just to remind you you're in Cuba, and that Cuba's in the past.

But to backtrack a little, before we hit the 12 miles (20km) of uninterrupted beach at Varadero we stopped off at the little town of San Miguel de los Banos, just a short drive off our route south of Colesio, where the ruined Gran Hotel stands in splendid desolation. The town was once an upmarket spa resort, yet it was not the revolution that killed it off, but rather pollution from a nearby sugar works poisoning the water supply.

It's not a ghost town, San Miguel, and there are poor but very friendly people living in what were once other fine hotels. But the Gran Hotel itself is empty, except for some bad-tempered bees that have nested in the ceiling of the entrance hall. We spent some time wandering around this crumbling husk of a building, with not another person in sight. It was one of the highlights of the trip, and it also seemed a metaphor for the country. Walking through this dilapidated, and slightly dangerous, old hotel you can't help think that it might one day be renovated. But then you also think that that would be a shame, and in a way the same applies to the country. Or to put it another way; the time to do a Cuban road trip is right now.

PLANNING NOTES

Start and finish: Havana.
Distance: 901 miles (1,450km).
Time needed: 11 days, including a couple in Havana before we set out, was ample.
When to go: Prices are highest around Christmas and the New Year while the low season is May, June and September. If a hurricane hits it tends to be between June and November and this is when there's also a higher chance of rain.
Vehicle: Although some say hiring a car is very difficult in Cuba, this is simply not the case; although at the time of writing there was still a shortage so you do need to book ahead and do this early. Be aware of add-ons, too, such as a returnable *cash* deposit of 200 CUCs (the tourist currency which operates alongside the local peso) and an obligatory 20 CUC a day insurance, both of which will need to be paid on picking up the car.
Beware of: In Cuba your hire car is likely to run on gasoline but never ask for 'petrol' at a service station as you will be given diesel. It's always 'gasolina especial', which is a 94 octane fuel. Oh, and if you are stuck behind a 1950s truck then make sure your windows are shut – the fumes will take years off your life.
Detours, extensions and variations: Lasso the loop out further east to take in the fine city of Camagüey.

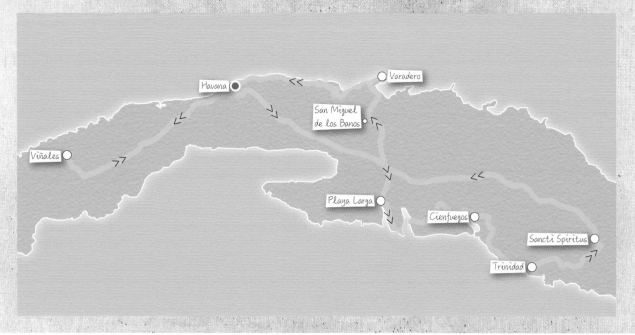

▲ **Road running through the Valle de la Luna near San Pedro de Atacama.** *(Bresmedia)*

▼ **A steam locomotive lies abandoned in the atmospheric ghost town of Humberstone.** *(Bresmedia)*

It's a slender country, Chile, squeezed very long and thin by the vast Pacific to the west and the majestic Andes to the east. This makes it quite difficult for road trip loops, and with hire car drop-off fees on the steep side it can be tricky to come up with a good linear route, too. Also, unless you have plenty of time one thing is certain: you need to choose between the north and the south.

In the north it's mostly about the Atacama Desert, and an ideal trip would be Arica, up close to the Peruvian border on the coast, down to the capital, Santiago. But as we did not have too much time we opted for a shorter version, basically following the northern Chilean stretch of the Pan-American Highway (Ruta 5) from Arica to San Pedro de Atacama.

Arica is a laid-back sort of place where pelicans scoop their prey from the sea and fish that escape the birds end up on plates in the restaurants that cling to the shoreline; it's a nice place to spend a night, but it's always good to get on the road. Starting the drive from sea level it's inevitable you will soon be climbing, but it seems more up and down to begin with, with rocky valley floors and twisting roads, before you hit those long, straight, mirage-pinched desert roads you've been dreaming of.

Our first stop was Iquique, but before this we visited the ghost town of Humberstone, which once served a now long-closed nitrate mine. It's a thought-provoking place. Ghost towns, like deserts themselves, serve to remind us of our place as specks in time and space; and also that the desert always wins.

Iquique itself has lovely light, which plays off the colourful buildings like visual music close to sundown. All the guidebooks say you need to fill up here as Calama is close to 250 miles (400km) away and there are no fuel stops in between. They are right, there's nothing much of anything in fact, except mile after glorious mile of empty desert, before you really start to feel you're climbing and then the Andes come into view beyond Calama on the road to San Pedro de Atacama (to finish we doubled back to Calama airport).

There's something special about the desert around the small frontier-feeling town of San Pedro de Atacama, with its backdrop of snowy mountains. The moonlike landscape of the Valle de la Luna should not be missed, and make sure you drive the salt road down to the surreal Laguna Chaxa to watch flamingos sipping their reflections. Also, check out the psychedelic rock formations in Rainbow Valley, and don't forget to glance up at the sugary night sky, oh and visit lovely Tocanao and…. Hold on; did I really say the Atacama was empty?

BY THE WAY ...

Shrining through

While roadside shrines presumably have a spiritual significance, they're also a great prompt for taking your foot off the gas, or a wake-up if you're beginning to flag during a long desert drive. Potential lifesavers then. In Chile these can be simple – a wooden box and cross and a photo – or a little bit more elaborate, with whole shacks full of pictures of the deceased along with their football shirts, guitars and other belongings. But the one that sticks in the memory is this, just off the road between Calama and San Pedro de Atacama, not least because of the questions it raises. Was he driving another car when he had the accident? Was he a passenger? Was he run over while crossing the road? Whatever the reason, he obviously loved his car and his parents or friends thought it was the ideal way to mark

a life sadly cut short. I wonder how long it will last, in the dry desert air? There's no rain so it's unlikely to rust away, so maybe it will save many a life over the coming decades as drivers slow to wonder why.

PLANNING NOTES

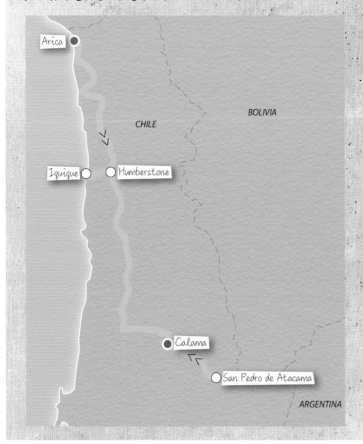

Start and finish: Arica to Calama.

Distance: 497 miles (800km).

Time needed: This was just a week, but make sure you spend a day or two in Santiago as it's a marvellous city – you will probably fly there and then back at the start and end of your road trip.

When to go: The Norte Grande is a year-round destination.

Vehicle: We used a Toyota Rav 4 but the main advantage of this was its big fuel tank rather than the 4wd, as that's not really needed on this trip.

Beware of: Petrol stations are few and far between so fill up when you can and carry plenty of water – the Atacama is the driest desert in the world.

Detours, extensions and variations: From Arica drive to the Codpa Valley, then on to Putre – via Timar and Tignamar – and then the Lauca National Park, and back to Arica on the amazing Ruta 11, for stunning mountain scenery, picturesque villages and wildlife.

Ruta 40 is one of the world's great road trips. Here are some numbers to help convince you. It's more than 3,100 miles (5,000km) long and it goes through 20 national parks; there's 27 Andean passes and 236 bridges to cross, while it climbs to a literally breathtaking altitude of around 5,000m (16,400ft), that giddy height reached at Abra del Acay in Salta Province.

On top of that (can you get on top of that in a car?) you see an awful lot of Argentina, as Ruta 40 cuts through the provinces of Santa Cruz, Chubut, Río Negro, Neuquen, Mendoza, San Juan, La Rioja, Catamarca, Tucumán, Salta and Jujuy as it runs north, paralleling the stark Andean spine of South America.

But this is a serious undertaking and you will need to be prepared. At the time of writing some stretches are still gravel – though the Argentinian government has woken up to the tourism benefits and it is gradually asphalting it – and even some of the paved sections, in more remote areas, are not in great condition. Also, on the long Patagonian stretches you need to be ready for strong winds that whistle across the

▼ Ruta 40 runs the length of Argentina and is one of the world's classic road trips. *(Shutterstock)*

▶ **The Perito Mereno Glacier is within easy reach of El Calafate and is pretty much a must-do detour from Ruta 40.** *(Shutterstock)*

plains, especially if you're in a motorhome or camper. But it's not all long straight roads by any means and there are some hairpin-heavy passes to negotiate, too.

You will also need to make sure your vehicle is up to it and if you're hiring – and the astronomical drop-off fees might scupper that plan – then while a 4x4 isn't necessarily required the bigger the fuel tank the better, as there are huge distances between petrol stations on some of the more remote sections of the road.

Highlights along the way, or close enough for a detour, are way too numerous to list but you wouldn't want to miss the Perito Mereno Glacier, to see and hear the ice splitting; Welsh tea in Trevelin; the Ruta de los Siete Lagos – a road trip in its own right – Mendoza, which is Argentina's wine centre, and the colourful rock-scapes of Quedraba de Humahuaca.

Ruta 40 has been called Argentina's Route 66, but in truth there's much more to it than that; this is not just an experience, it is a great adventure.

PLANNING NOTES

Start and finish: Punta Loyola near Rio Gallegos in Santa Cruz Province (south) to La Quiaca in Jujuy Province (north).

Distance: 3,100 miles (5,000km).

Time needed: A month would be ideal, but there's enough to see and do to fill two or more.

When to go: December to March – summer in the southern hemisphere.

Vehicle: While it's doable in a regular car something tough would be better, and the chunky tyres of a 4x4 will at least help prevent punctures. Renting a car is problematic, with the drop-off fees, so buying locally might make sense, although that can be complicated. Shipping your own vehicle in through Chile is possible, but expensive.

Beware of: The more lonely parts of this route are very remote and you will need to fill up at every opportunity, even if that means – and it could – queueing to do so. Take extra fuel if you can and also food, as there are few shops in some areas. Also, make sure you have enough cash; not everywhere will take cards and you can't rely on the ATMs.

Detours, extensions and variations: To beat the drop-off fees why not consider driving a portion there-and-back? Or take the RN3 north from Rio Gallegos to Trelew, then drive to Ruta 40 via Ruta 25, which crosses the Patagonian steppe, before heading south to complete the loop.

from the state of Rio Grande do Norte in the north-east to Rio Grande do Sul, the state that is furthest south.

▲ The stretch of coast road between Rio and Angra dos Reis – it's easy to see why this is called the Costa Verde. *(Shutterstock)*

Between the cities of Rio de Janeiro and São Paulo – both noisy, intense and exciting in their own particular ways – runs a portion of the BR-101, and a drive that will take you along the Costa Verde – the green coast. When I say a 'portion', it's quite a small serving, as the BR-101 actually runs right down the Brazilian coast for almost 3,000 miles (4,800km)

The stretch we're interested in is just 370 miles (600km) or so, but they're miles packed with wonderful beaches, characterful towns and achingly verdant forest – while a deep blue sea chipped with sunlight and flecked with white waves is never too far from the road. To put it another way, it's quite nice.

There's Rio to negotiate first, though, and then you follow the 101 until you hit the coast near Ilha de Madeira, before reaching Angra dos Reis, about 93 miles (150km) from Rio. You'll have to leave the car behind if you want to visit nearby Ilha Grande, as there are no roads or motor vehicles on this island paradise; though it's not always been thought of as such as it was once home to a leper colony. Tourism has picked up a little since…

▲ You won't be allowed to take your vehicle into the cobble-clad historic streets of Paraty – unless it's horse-drawn. *(Shutterstock)*

Further down the coast is what's perhaps the main event on this road trip, Paraty. This is surrounded by jungle-quilted mountains that rise as high as 1,300m (4,265ft) and it is a real gem, a UNESCO World Heritage site that will give you a real flavour of colonial Brazil.

From Paraty the road twists into the hills as it heads towards Ubatuba, and miles and miles of beaches. If surfing, or lying on the sand, is not for you, then there's always the Serra do Mar National Park – with walking, waterfalls and wildlife.

Other stops worth considering are São Sebastião – with its well-preserved colonial centre – and the beautiful island of Ilhabela, the hangout of the São Paulo well-to-do, before this stretch of the BR-101 finishes at Santos. This port town is perhaps best known for its part in the story of Brazil's favourite son, Pele, who played for Santos FC for most of his career. There's a museum dedicated to the great player in the town.

Another Brazilian sporting great, Ayrton Senna, came from São Paulo, which marks the end of this trip. One thing you might find is that while hardly any Brazilians think they're Pele, almost every Brazilian who gets behind the wheel thinks they're Senna. Bear that in mind on the road. That said, São Paulo is a surprisingly easy city to drive in.

PLANNING NOTES

Start and finish: Rio de Janeiro to São Paulo (Rio and São Paulo airports are about 267 miles (430km) apart, so you could make this a loop using the BR-116 highway).
Distance: 373 miles (600km)
Time needed: You will want to spend a little time in Rio before setting out, and maybe a day in São Paulo at the end, but it's a short drive so a week or so would suffice.
When to go: It's warm or hot all year round, but a place this green also gets a bit of rain; especially from October to January.

Vehicle: Brazilian roads aren't too bad and this one is fine for a regular hire car. Renting a car in Brazil is straightforward, though it can be difficult to find an automatic.
Beware of: Be careful in the cities and avoid areas where there's a high risk of theft (do some research before you travel). But don't let this put you off; with a few sensible precautions you should be fine.
Detours, extensions and variations: A nice detour on the way from Santos to São Paulo is Paranapiacaba, a late-19th century British-built railway village that is in a remarkable state of preservation.

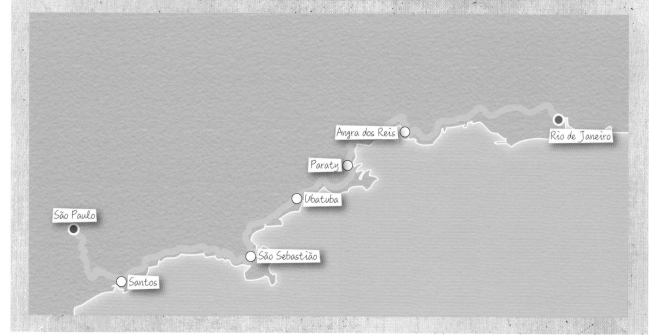

▲ The road to Arenal and La Fortuna – if you like jungle, you'll love Costa Rica. *(Shutterstock)*

This Central American country has become a popular destination, and with its majestic mountains and exotic forests, not to mention both Caribbean and Pacific beaches – one of the advantages of travelling to the pinch point of the Americas – it's not difficult to see why.

Most will arrive at Juan Santamaria International Airport, close to the capital of San Jose and a perfect jumping-off point for a road trip that will showcase every facet of this lovely little country.

If you leave exploring the hectic capital until the end of the trip then the first stop would be the unmissable Arenal Volcano National Park, near La Fortuna; which not only features a properly smoking volcano but is also packed with wildlife and offers plenty of exciting activities (don't miss the La Fortuna waterfall).

Next stop is the Monteverde Cloud Forest, one of the best places to get a feel for Costa Rica's flora and fauna – there are over 100 mammal species, 400 bird, and thousands of different types of plant. But beyond that this place has a unique atmosphere – well, it is often in a cloud! – best experienced from up high on the canopy walkways.

Taking your head out of the clouds it's time to hit the coast at the lively beach town of Tamarindo, from where you can head south to Malpais, a secluded fishing village where the rich and famous have built holiday homes, Mel Gibson

◄ Now that's what I call a road trip! A rather contented-looking sloth in Manuel Antonio National Park. *(Shutterstock)*

among them. Santa Teresa and Montezuma are also cool places to stop.

Taking the ferry from Playa Naranjo – a pleasant voyage of around an hour – to Punta Arenas, the route then continues down the coast to Jaco (a tourist hotspot, so not to everyone's taste) and then Costa Rica's most popular national park, Parque Nacional Manuel Antonio, where all that keeps the rainforest from tumbling into the sea is the exquisite beaches.

Looping back around to San Jose by way of San Isidro del General – visiting the fabulous double-tiered Nauyaca Waterfalls, near Dominical, on the way – you can also take in the interesting coffee-growing area just south of the capital; most of the plantations offer tours, not to mention a very good cup of coffee.

PLANNING NOTES

Start and finish: San Jose or Juan Santamaria International Airport.
Distance: 655 miles (1,055km).
Time needed: Ten days to two weeks.
When to go: Some roads can be impassable during the rainy season (August to October), but on the other hand there are fewer tourists and you can work around the daily 2pm deluge. December to April is best, but you might need to book ahead.
Vehicle: Some of the roads are quite poor and to get into the parks a 4wd is the best bet – many rental agencies will stipulate that you use one in the rainy season anyway.
Beware of: You will be well advised to seek local advice on the state of the roads, especially during the wet season. And avoid driving at night.
Detours, extensions and variations: The Caribbean coast also has lots to offer and the beaches and parks to the east are well worth a visit. Or extend the loop further south to Parque Nacional Corcovado for one of the best unspoilt tracts of rainforest in Central America.

▲ The Carretera Austral in Chile is one of the great driving adventures. *(Shutterstock)*

▼ The Hanging Glacier of Queulat National Park is just one of the natural wonders close to the Carretera Austral. *(Shutterstock)*

Also known as Ruta 7, the Carretera Austral runs south through northern Patagonia from Puerto Montt to Villa O'Higgins on the Argentinian border. It is a journey of forests and lakes, mountains and glaciers, and remote settlements. Not all of it is paved and there are many gravel stretches – at the time of writing the asphalt petered out just beyond Villa Cerro Castillo – seriously potholed sections and, especially towards the end, filling-loosening corrugations. At the top end, wet weather can cause landslides and some of the ferry crossings along the route need to be booked in advance. There are some great camping spots along the way, but you will need to stock up on supplies before you set off. In short, this trip will need a little planning.

Staggering natural beauty is a feature of this classic South American adventure, and some standout highlights as you head south include Parque Pumalin (forests and waterfalls, hiking and hot pools); white water rafting in the Futaleufú Valley (which early settlers called a 'landscape painted by God'); Ventisquero Colgante (the hanging glacier); the mighty Saltos del Cóndor waterfall; the thermal baths at Termas de Puyuhuapi; the idyllic village of Puerto Rio Tranquilo on the shore of Lago General Carrera (close to the Capilla de Mármal, a striking limestone cliff pocked with caves that boats can enter); Parque Patagonia (for awesome hiking); and finally the end of the road at Villa O'Higgins – a place that you could only reach by small plane or boat until 1999. Which just about sums this trip up. If you want remote, then this is for you.

PLANNING NOTES

Start and finish: Puerto Montt to Villa O'Higgins (though for practical reasons this might need to be done as a there-and-back trip, see below).

Distance: 760 miles (1,223km); or 1,520 miles (2,446km) there-and-back.

Time needed: It's not a huge distance but the going's not always good and if you want to see all this has to offer, and travel back to Puerto Montt, you're looking at three weeks at least.

When to go: Between October and April, with high season from December to March. Note: there's a chance of bad weather at any time of the year.

Vehicle: While it's said to be possible to do this in a regular car good ground clearance would be advised, which really means a 4x4 or a pickup truck (some rental agencies will insist on these if you say you're driving this route).

Beware of: Hire car drop-off fees are on the large side, which makes a there-and-back trip the best bet, maybe saving some sights for the return leg. Most settlements along the route have petrol stations but mobile phone coverage is sparse and don't expect to find an internet connection in some of the towns.

Detours, extensions and variations: Puerto Montt is a great base for exploring the beautiful Chilean Lake District to its north.

The advice is not to drive at night; which might instantly bring to mind holdups and carjackings, such has been the reputation of Mexico in recent years. But the real reason is a little more mundane – although arguably no less dangerous – animals, and their maddening lack of road sense. Hit a cow and you'll know about it.

Beyond steering around steers, the mostly two-lane Carretera Transpeninsular (also known as Transpeninsula Highway, Federal Highway 1 and Ruta 1), which runs the length of the Baja Peninsula in Mexican California, is a doable, enjoyable and exciting road trip. It starts in Tijuana on the US border and ends in Los Cabos at the tip of the peninsula, and manages to take in both the Pacific and the Sea of Cortez coastlines along the way.

It's worth spending a day or two in Tijuana to begin with,

▲ If you like your roads straight and fringed with cowboy film cacti then there are parts of Baja's Carretera Transpeninsular that will be right up your ruta. *(Shutterstock)*

to get used to Mexico if nothing else. It also makes sense to hire a car here rather than bringing one from the US, and then having to negotiate what's said to be the world's busiest border crossing.

Heading south, Ensenada is known for its vineyards and there are other activities and sights too – including the spectacular sea spout at nearby La Bufadora – before the journey turns into the opening sequence of a western for a day or two, with nothing much to see in the desert but giant cacti – iconic road trip country, then. For 250 miles (400km) beyond El Rosario there's not much fuel to be had, so fill up there.

Guerrero Negro is great for whale watching and you can get *very* close to the huge Californian grey whales here, while the oasis town of San Ignacio is a good base for this, too. Mulegé is also worth a stop (with some of Mexico's best beaches nearby), before lovely Loreto; and the interesting state capital of La Paz. The end of the road is Los Cabos, well-known for its beach resorts such as Cabo San Lucas, which has been described as a 'miniature Acapulco'.

This drive might sound idyllic, and in many ways it is, but you need to keep your wits about you. It's a dangerous road, seemingly in constant repair and with little in the way of guardrails, while it's also very narrow in places; causing an involuntary sharp intake of breath when a huge truck is travelling at speed in the opposite direction. But it's not all long desert roads and there are some twisting mountain sections to contend with, too. In that respect the Carretera Transpeninsular certainly ticks lots of road trip boxes.

▼ After a long, hot drive you'll be rewarded with stunning coastal scenery in Cabo San Lucas. *(Shutterstock)*

PLANNING NOTES

Start and finish: Tijuana to Los Cabos.

Distance: 1,037 miles (1,670km).

Time needed: A week or more; depending on how long you want to stay at each stop.

When to go: If you're keen on seeing whales then January to the end of March is best but otherwise Baja is a year-round destination.

Vehicle: Pick up a hire car in Tijuana and drop it off at Cabo San Lucas. There will be a drop-off fee, but it usually works out cheaper than driving all the way back.

Beware of: This road suffers from a blight of speed bumps – called topes – as the authorities try to stem the proliferation of roadside shrines. Watch out for them.

Detours, extensions and variations: Fork east before you reach Punta Prieta towards Bahía de los Ángeles, which is in the lovely bay of the same name. It's a peaceful spot, but if you want a little action it's also great for sports fishing and diving.

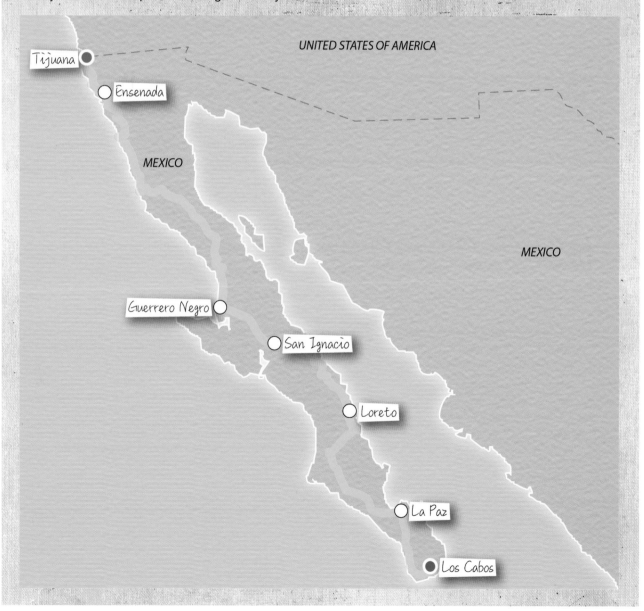

UNITED STATES OF AMERICA

Tijuana

Ensenada

MEXICO

MEXICO

Guerrero Negro

San Ignacio

Loreto

La Paz

Los Cabos

ROAD TRIP CHECKLIST

For the car
- ☐ Car serviced
- ☐ Check fluid levels including engine oil and gearbox oil; brake fluid; water; windscreen washer
- ☐ Check condition of tyres; wiper blades; hoses; belts; lights
- ☐ Full tank of fuel
- ☐ Can of oil; spare light bulbs; gaffer tape; basic tool kit for small jobs
- ☐ Country identification sticker if not on number plate (GB, for example)

For the driver and passengers
- ☐ Good-quality sunglasses for driving
- ☐ Sun cream
- ☐ Snacks (sweet and savoury – nuts and dried fruit; energy bars etc.)
- ☐ Big bag of sweets (optional)
- ☐ Water (plenty) in big bottles, with small bottles/mugs to drink from
- ☐ Phone/device charger and plug socket adapter
- ☐ Travel insurance
- ☐ Foreign currency
- ☐ Check you can use credit/debit card in country visiting
- ☐ Bag for rubbish
- ☐ Camera (in a place where it can easily be reached)

For the cops and the bureaucrats
- ☐ Passports/visas
- ☐ Inoculation certificate (if required)
- ☐ Driving licence (and International Driving Permit if required)
- ☐ Proof of vehicle ownership or permission (V5c, VE103 forms etc. Also, carnet if required)
- ☐ Car insurance (green card if required)
- ☐ Car insurance contact numbers
- ☐ Vignette (if required)
- ☐ Sense of humour and two jars of patience

For the journey
- ☐ Maps/road atlas
- ☐ Satnav (if separate) and charger
- ☐ Downloaded apps like maps.me on phone
- ☐ Road book including printed-out directions
- ☐ Guidebook
- ☐ Print-offs of accommodation confirmation

For the unexpected
- ☐ First aid kit (and painkillers etc.)
- ☐ Useful telephone numbers
- ☐ Smartphone and charger
- ☐ Toilet roll
- ☐ High vis vest (mandatory in some countries)
- ☐ Warning triangle (ditto)
- ☐ Decoy wallet (if required)
- ☐ Breakdown recovery contact details
- ☐ Torch
- ☐ Travel rug or blanket

For the hire car
- ☐ Inspect car
- ☐ Check spare tyre and jack
- ☐ Make sure you know how to put it in 4wd if applicable
- ☐ Check terms and conditions
- ☐ Who pays for tolls and how?
- ☐ Petrol or diesel?
- ☐ Where is petrol cap and how does it open?
- ☐ Excess insurance

For the campsite
- ☐ Tent, sleeping bag etc.
- ☐ Small packs of vital ingredients (salt, pepper, chilli powder, etc.)
- ☐ Corkscrew/bottle opener
- ☐ Something to sit on; table (more important than you might think)
- ☐ Towels (easy to forget if you usually stay in hotels)
- ☐ Torch and headlights

For the fun
- ☐ Mascot
- ☐ Playlist/CDs/talking books
- ☐ Games for kids (and the kids, if you have them)
- ☐ Sick bags (see above)